HOW TO DO
just about
ANYTHING IN
Microsoft®
Word

Reader's Digest
HOW TO DO just about ANYTHING IN
Microsoft®
Word

Published by The Reader's Digest Association Limited
London • New York • Sydney • Montreal

How to do just about anything in Microsoft® Word

was edited and designed by The Reader's Digest Association Limited, London

First edition Copyright ©2001
The Reader's Digest Association Limited,
11 Westferry Circus, Canary Wharf, London E14 4HE
www.readersdigest.co.uk

Paperback edition 2005

We are committed to both the quality of our products and the service we provide to our customers.
We value your comments, so please feel free to contact us on 08705 113366,
or via our website at: www.readersdigest.co.uk
If you have any comments or suggestions about this book, e-mail us at:
gbeditorial@readersdigest.co.uk

Printing and binding: Toppan Printing Company, Hong Kong

Contents

How to use this book 8

Set up your PC safely 10

What is Word? 12

Basics

Explore the program 16

Entering text 20

Save your work 22

Print your work 24

Styling Your Document

Format a document 34

Format a paragraph 36

Using columns and bullets 38

Using tabs 40

Design a letterhead 42

AutoFormat your text 46

Using tables 48

Wizards and templates 50

Headers and footers 52

Inserting text breaks 54

Styling Your Text

Choose and size a font 28

Style and colour text 30

Editing Text

Cut, copy and paste 56

Spelling and grammar 58

Thesaurus and Word Count 60

AutoCorrect your text 62

Find and replace 64

Customising Word

Change your preferences 66

Edit a toolbar 68

Viewing options 72

Using Graphics

Add a picture 74

Create a family newsletter 76

WordArt and AutoShape 80

Add a background 82

Special Functions

Mail Merge 84

Make address labels 86

Use macros 90

Sort a list 92

Doing a calculation 94

Import and export files 96

Set up a family Web site 98

Glossary 104

Index 108

Acknowledgments 112

How to use this book

This book is a fun and approachable guide to mastering Microsoft Word. All the most useful features of the program are clearly set out as step-by-step projects, with pictures that show you exactly what you will see on screen. Unlike a manual, you'll never find yourself wondering how to complete a task or having to unravel complicated instructions.

GETTING AROUND THE BOOK
This book covers the main features of Word. You can either read it from start to finish, or dip in and out, as you wish.

Basics
Are you completely new to Word? Learn how to create, save and print your first ever document.

Customising Word
Word's automatic settings dictate how you work. Find out how to set your own preferences.

Styling text
You can style text to suit all kinds of documents, from formal letters to party invitations. Discover the typefaces and how to size and style them.

Styling your document
Word is an extremely versatile program. Learn how to make your newsletter look professional, use columns of text, set indents on paragraphs, create stylish borders and lots more.

Editing text
With just a few key strokes, you can select and move whole paragraphs of text, and search for and replace words or phrases. Thanks to Word's spellchecker and thesaurus, you can also ensure that your documents are always word perfect.

Using graphics
A picture can be worth a thousand words. Using colour, ClipArt, photos and other graphic features, make your documents even more inviting to read.

Special functions
Welcome to the Word masterclass! Here you can find out how to do some of the more challenging tasks, such as creating mail merges or Web pages. These fun and useful functions are simpler than you might expect.

WHICH VERSION OF WORD?
The information in this book is based on a PC using Word 2003. If you have an earlier version of Word, you'll find that it looks different, but the functions explained in these pages are very similar or even identical.

Close up
These project-related tips offer you extra detail on various Word functions.

Key word
You'll find handy definitions of technical words or phrases here.

Bright idea
Wondering how to use your new-found skills? Look out for these tips.

GETTING AROUND THE PAGE

You're guided through every task in this book by means of illustrated steps and a range of visual features. Here are the key elements to look for on each page.

See also
Want to find out more? This panel points you towards other relevant projects for you to try.

Step-by-step
Projects are set out in clear steps. You are instructed on the keyboard and mouse commands to give, and which files and menus to access.

Useful tips
Near the main block of text are explanations of the more complex aspects of a task and alternative ways to do things.

Before you start
Projects begin with a small section of text to read. This outlines points to consider and anything you need to do before you begin.

Snapshots
Pictures of the PC screen – 'snapshots' – show you what you'll see on your own screen at each stage of the project.

Annotations
Sometimes a specific part of a step-by-step will be focused on and explained in greater depth.

Magnifications
Snapshots of the PC screen that require special attention are magnified so that you can see them more clearly.

Type in quotes
Words inside quotation marks are either the exact words you will see on screen, or what you need to type in yourself as part of a step.

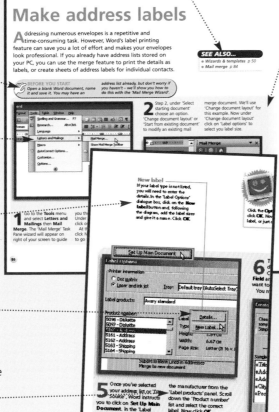

Bold type
Any bold text is a command for you to carry out. You might need to select a menu option, a toolbar button, a dialogue box tab or press a key.

Page turns
The yellow arrow indicates that your project continues over the page. The features in this book range from two pages to six.

Watch out
These tips will warn you of things to look out for that can cause a project to go wrong, and give advice on how to avoid them.

Expert advice
Advanced tips and guidance to enable you to get professional looking results from all of Word's facilities.

That's amazing!
Inspiring ideas and explanations, such as time-saving shortcuts, which you will find both interesting and useful.

Set up your PC safely

When you are choosing where you want to put your PC, check that there is adequate space and several mains sockets for all the equipment. You need to consider lighting and seating, and the amount of desk space available. If you want to send faxes from your computer or connect to the Internet, you will also need to be near a telephone wall socket.

SITTING AT YOUR COMPUTER

You need to think carefully about how to arrange your area, as a poorly laid out computer desk and PC will be irritating and may prevent you from using your computer properly.

If you find yourself leaning towards the monitor, increase the scale at which you are viewing your document.

Your legs should remain uncrossed and your knees should be lower than your hips.

An adjustable chair will support your back and can be altered to suit each family user.

Your feet should rest flat on the floor.

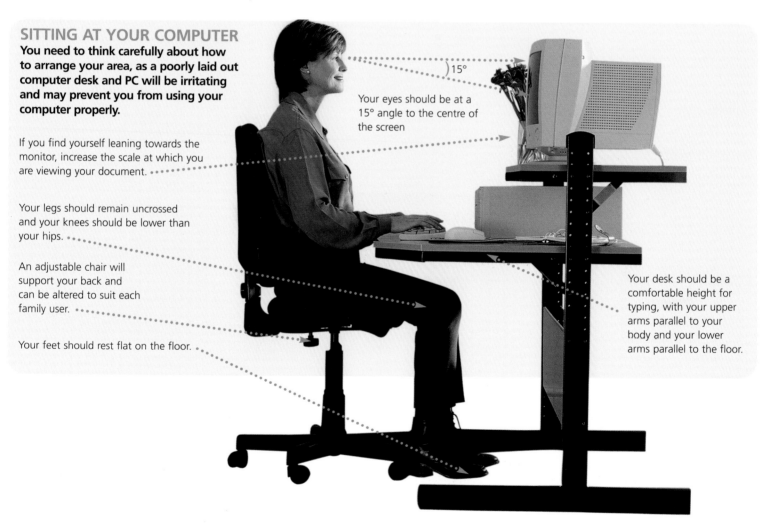

15°

Your eyes should be at a 15° angle to the centre of the screen

Your desk should be a comfortable height for typing, with your upper arms parallel to your body and your lower arms parallel to the floor.

NAMING AND PLACING PARTS

Your PC's hardware comprises all the parts that you can actually see and handle. Knowing exactly where to place these elements ensures a safe and efficient work area.

Monitor

This houses the computer screen. Position your monitor to avoid reflections, but do not face a bright window yourself as this may lead to eyestrain.

System unit

This is the part of your computer that connects everything together. Leave space so that you can plug in the cables easily and to allow for ventilation. Don't leave cables trailing.

Mouse

Place the mouse to the side of your keyboard that suits whether you are left- or right-handed. Use a mouse mat to create the correct amount of friction for the mouse, and be sure there is plenty of room to move the mouse.

External speakers

For the best sound quality, speakers should be well spaced apart at desk level or higher, not just pushed under the desk. Ensure that the computer is situated so that others are not disturbed by computer games or alert sounds.

Keyboard

Make sure the keyboard is on a stable and level surface within easy reach. Leave enough space in front for hands and wrists. Ensure that the desk is at the correct height.

Printer

Position your printer near the system unit. Make sure there is sufficient space around it for loading the paper trays.

Expert advice

If you are planning to use your computer a lot, either surfing the Internet or doing your accounts and letters, then you should invest in a good quality comfortable office chair. Most dining chairs do not offer the support for your back that is so important when you are sitting still for long periods. Also, most office chairs are adjustable, so it will suit every member of the family. Remember, even with a comfortable chair, you should take regular 10 minute breaks to walk around.

What is Word?

Word processors are programs that enable you to create, save and print documents. Once you have created a document, you can re-use it as often as you like, making any changes and corrections you wish. Word is one of the most versatile word processors available. It makes editing and styling your documents quick, easy and fun.

SEE ALSO...
- *Explore the program* p 16
- *Entering text* p 20
- *Style your text* p 30
- *Edit a toolbar* p 68

WHAT YOU CAN DO

Word offers you an impressive range of options to help make your documents look good and save you time.

Choose from a wide range of typefaces, known as 'fonts', which you can set in different sizes, styles – such as bold, italic or underline – and colours. You can even use special effects, so the text sparkles or flashes, for example.

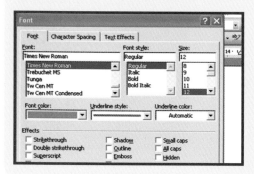

Design your page

You can set your document to the page size that suits you, choose the size of the margins, how text is aligned, and whether you want it in columns. You can insert boxes and tables, set paragraph indents, and add bullet points or automatically number lists. If you want to illustrate your text, there is a huge library of ClipArt available, or you can insert your own illustrations and photographs.

Work faster with templates

If you're not so keen on setting up documents from scratch, try using Word's ready-made templates instead. These include letterheads, memos, faxes and Web page templates.

Word perfect

Word's Spelling and Grammar facility alerts you to misspelt words and badly constructed sentences. If you're stuck for an alternative word, try using the Thesaurus.

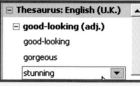

Saving time

If you need to do a mail shot, the Mail Merge facility is a must. Create your letter with gaps for information, such as names and addresses. Then using Word's step-by-step guide merge the letter with data records created in Word or imported from a database.

Word and the Office suite

Although you can buy Word 2003 as a separate program, it usually comes as one of a suite of programs, collectively named 'Microsoft Office'. The software programs bundled in Office vary, depending on which version you buy. The basic version – 'Microsoft Office for Small Businesses' – includes Excel, which is a spreadsheet program, and Outlook, an information management program that also allows you to send and receive e-mails. The more expensive 'Office Professional' also includes PowerPoint for creating on-screen presentations with sound and animation, and Access, a powerful database package.

GETTING AROUND IN WORD

If this is your first time using a word processing program, you'll need a few tips to get you started.

Using the mouse

You use the mouse to point at different areas of the screen and to issue commands. It is designed to sit comfortably under your hand, with your index finger poised over the left button. You will mostly click with the left button, but sometimes you'll need to use the right. When you are following the instructions in this book, 'clicking' the mouse refers to the left button. If you need to use the right, you'll be told to 'right-click'.

When you move the mouse over text on screen, it changes from a white selection arrow

to the insertion point, which looks like a capital I (see left). If you want to enter text, click the insertion point where you want it and type. To select a

button on a toolbar or a menu at the top of the screen, point the selection arrow and click. Double-clicking the left mouse button is a speedy way to select and confirm an option.

Selecting text

To select a whole line of text, position the arrow over the white area on the left of your document,

next to your chosen line, and left-click once. It will be highlighted instantly. To select more, or less, than one line, left-click in front of the first character and, with the button held down, drag the mouse over the text as far up, down, left or right as you require. Release the button when you have selected all the text you want. This is known as 'click and drag'.

To select just one word, double-click on it with your left mouse button. If you click three times,

you select the whole paragraph. Once you have selected an area of text, you can style it, change font or font size, copy and paste it into another part of the document, or delete it.

Moving around the page

You can scroll through your document by clicking on the arrows at either end of the scroll bars to the right and along the bottom of the screen, or by dragging the grey block on the scroll bar up or down.

Menus, toolbars and commands

You can issue instructions in three ways – using menus, using the toolbars or using shortcut keys.
Menus: If you're new to Word, it's a good idea to use the menus until you are more familiar with the program (see page 18). The menus are at the

very top of the window, and from them you can style, save and print your document, among other things.
Toolbars: Some of the most common commands appear as buttons on the toolbars. Although they provide a quick route to the same end result, such as aligning or emboldening your selected text, and saving or opening a new document, they do not offer the flexibility of the

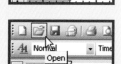

menu alternatives, which often open up dialogue boxes containing a wider variety of options (see page 18).
Key commands: Shortcut keys are a combination of two or three keystrokes and are useful for people who prefer using the keyboard to the mouse (see overleaf).

Close up
Using Word 2003, you can open a document that has been created in an older version of Word. However, you cannot use an older version of Word to open a document created in Word 2003.

USING THE KEYBOARD

Function keys are shortcuts to commands:
F1 accesses Microsoft Help and Support.
F2 is for moving text. Select your text, press **F2**, click the point on your page where you wish the text to go to and press the **Return** key.
F4 repeats your last command.

F5 opens a dialogue box for 'Find' and 'Replace' features, and 'Go To', which enables you to jump to another part of your document.
F7 checks a document for spelling and grammar.
F12 Creates a duplicate version of your document using the 'Save As' feature.

Insert allows you to type over existing text.
Delete gets rid of any selected text or item.
Home places the cursor at the start of the line.
End places the cursor at the end of the line.
Page Up places the cursor at the top of the page.
Page Down places the cursor at the page bottom.

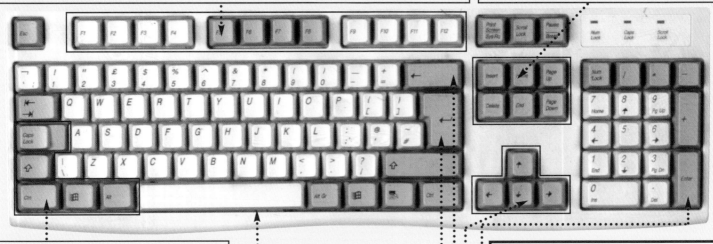

Caps Lock causes all the letters that you type to appear as capitals.
Shift allows you to type a letter on a key as a capital or to select the topmarked option on the key. For example, pressing 'Shift' + '5' types the '%' symbol.
Ctrl and **Alt** keys, when pressed in conjunction with other keys, access different commands (keyboard shortcuts). For example, 'Ctrl' + 'P' displays the 'Print' dialogue box.
Ctrl + Alt + Delete is a useful way to quit Word, should your screen freeze up.
Windows key Accesses the Start menu.

Spacebar adds spaces between words.

Return creates a paragraph break or ends a line early. ·····················

Backspace deletes text to the left of your cursor. ·····················

Arrow keys move the cursor up, down, left and right. ·····················

Enter key works like the Return key. ·········

Keyboard shortcuts

You can use all kinds of shortcuts to style your text, format your pages and access commands.

Ctrl + Shift + Spacebar creates a non-breaking space. This means that the words either side of the space are kept together on the same line.
Ctrl + Shift + hyphen creates a non-breaking hyphen. This means that a hyphenated word will not be split over two lines.
Ctrl + Q removes paragraph formatting.
Ctrl + Spacebar removes character formatting.
Ctrl + B makes text bold.
Ctrl + U underlines text.
Ctrl + I italicises text.
Ctrl + Shift + < decreases font size.
Ctrl + Shift + > increases font size.
Ctrl + F2 previews how your page will look when it is printed.
Ctrl + F4 closes the window you're working in.
Ctrl + F6 goes to the next open Word window.
Alt + F4 closes the Word program.
Alt + F8 runs a pre-recorded macro.
Alt + F10 maximises the Word window.

Close up
Use the Help menu to find out more about Word's function keys and shortcuts using Alt and Ctrl. Click the question mark icon on the toolbar and type in 'keyboard shortcuts'. Click Search.

Basics

Explore the program

Many people use Word more frequently than other programs. Although Word is designed to be intuitive, you will be able to use it more confidently and efficiently if you first take time to get to know the functions in the main document window. This will provide you with a better understanding of the many powerful features on offer.

SEE ALSO...
- *What is Word?* p 12
- *Entering text* p 20

BEFORE YOU START
You may have a shortcut for accessing Word on your computer Desktop. Look out for a 'Word' icon, with a small arrow in the bottom left-hand corner. Double-click on this to run Word.

2 As the program opens, you will see a title window appear briefly (below). This tells you which version of Word you are using. After a few seconds this window disappears and the program continues to load.

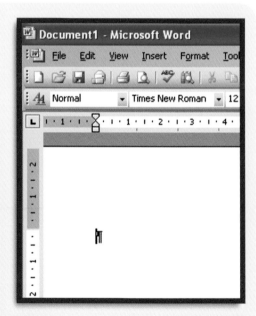

1 If you don't have a Desktop shortcut to Word, click on the **Start** button, if you have already used Word you will see it displayed in the start menu. Click on **Microsoft Office Word 2003** to run it. Alternatively, move the pointer to **All Programs** and select **Microsoft Office** then **Microsoft Office Word 2003**.

3 Next, a blank Word document appears on screen, into which you can start typing text. However, before you do this it is best to become acquainted with the window and the tools that you might want to use to manipulate your text.

THE DOCUMENT WINDOW

Commands for manipulating text and documents are listed on drop-down menus or presented as icons on buttons in the toolbars. Often there are different ways of accessing the same command.

Minimize button
Click here to reduce your document to a named button on the Taskbar at the bottom of the screen (see 'Minimized' button below).

Maximize/Restore button
This button enlarges the window, so it fills the screen. After maximising, the button looks like two overlapping boxes. Click again to restore the window to its previous size.

Close buttons
The upper button closes the program. The lower button closes the current document, but leaves the Word program running.

Title bar
Shows the name of the document in which you are working.

Menu bar
Drop-down menus of themed commands.

Standard toolbar
One-click buttons to activate common commands.

Formatting toolbar
Buttons and drop-down menus for formatting text.

Rulers
Shows you the width of your text area and any indents or tabs you have set. Clicking and sliding the small tabs along the ruler changes the setting. The vertical ruler shows your top and bottom print margins.

View buttons
Click on these to view your document in different formats, such as how it will look when it's printed or in a Web page format.

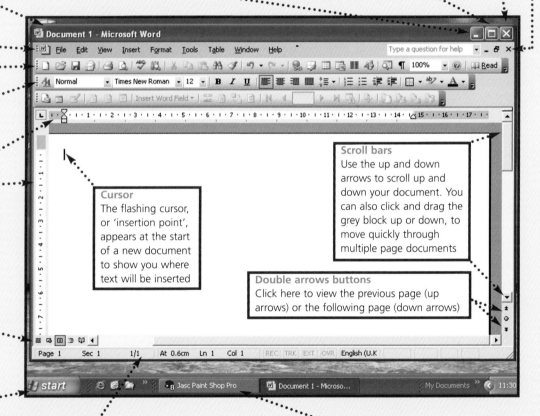

Cursor
The flashing cursor, or 'insertion point', appears at the start of a new document to show you where text will be inserted

Scroll bars
Use the up and down arrows to scroll up and down your document. You can also click and drag the grey block up or down, to move quickly through multiple page documents

Double arrows buttons
Click here to view the previous page (up arrows) or the following page (down arrows)

Taskbar
Contains the Start button and many useful shortcuts to your programs and settings.

Status bar
Shows the current status of your document. It tells you which page you are viewing and how many pages your document contains. It displays where you are on a page in centimetres, lines and columns.

'Minimized' button
Shows which other programs/documents are currently open. Here, 'Paint Shop Pro' has been minimised. Click on the button to restore the program or document.

THE MENU BAR

All the tasks you could want to perform in Word are listed on drop-down menus under the headings on the Menu bar.

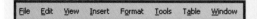

Before you start using Word, it's a good idea to click on each heading to familiarise yourself with the options. Some actions have icons beside them representing how the command buttons are displayed on the toolbars.

File

Commands in the File menu relate to the management of documents as a whole. Selecting 'New' creates a new document. You can also save, print and quickly open documents that you have recently worked on.

View

This menu contains commands which allow you to change how you view documents on screen and to see what they look like when they are printed, as well as to zoom in to see more detail or just to make it easier on your eyes. You can also insert headers and footers in your documents from here.

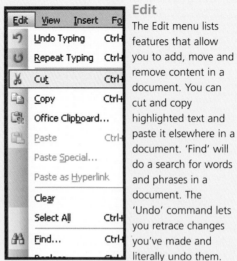

Edit

The Edit menu lists features that allow you to add, move and remove content in a document. You can cut and copy highlighted text and paste it elsewhere in a document. 'Find' will do a search for words and phrases in a document. The 'Undo' command lets you retrace changes you've made and literally undo them.

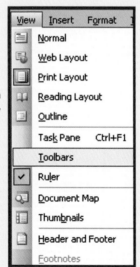

Format

This menu lists options for changing text – either individual letters or whole sections of text. You can alter paragraph settings, change the font and colour of the text and add borders. You can also select a preset style for your whole document.

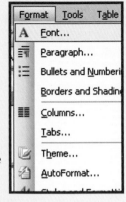

Tools

The Tools menu offers functions such as checking the spelling and grammar in your text. You can print envelopes using addresses from the contacts section of Microsoft Outlook. You can also customise buttons on the various toolbars from this menu.

Help

If you need help with Word or would like the friendly Office Assistant to help with a specific task, then select the option you want from this menu, including help on the Web.

Expert advice
If you aren't sure what all the icons on your PC mean, go to the **View** menu and select **Toolbars** then **Customize**. Click the **Options** tab. In the 'Other' section, tick the boxes 'Show ScreenTips on toolbars' and 'Show shortcut keys in ScreenTips'. Now, whenever you pass the pointer over an icon the ScreenTip will tell you what it does and what the keyboard shortcut is.

Close up
A double-headed arrow at the bottom of a menu means that further options are available. An arrow to the right of a command in any menu indicates a sub-menu of options. Click on either and the menu will extend.

THE STANDARD TOOLBAR

You will usually see this immediately below the Menu bar of your document. It contains a standardised set of useful command button icons which you can customise, adding the commands that you use frequently.

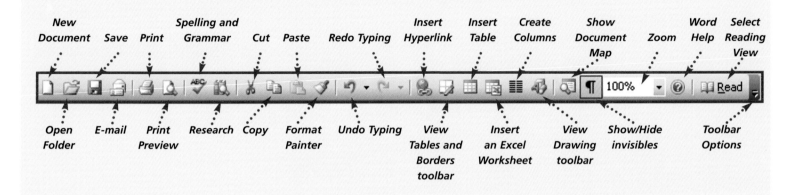

New Document · Save · Print · Spelling and Grammar · Cut · Paste · Redo Typing · Insert Hyperlink · Insert Table · Create Columns · Show Document Map · Zoom · Word Help · Select Reading View

Open Folder · E-mail · Print Preview · Research · Copy · Format Painter · Undo Typing · View Tables and Borders toolbar · Insert an Excel Worksheet · View Drawing toolbar · Show/Hide invisibles · Toolbar Options

THE FORMATTING TOOLBAR

Below the Standard toolbar in your document window you will usually see the Formatting toolbar. This contains a standardised set of useful command buttons.

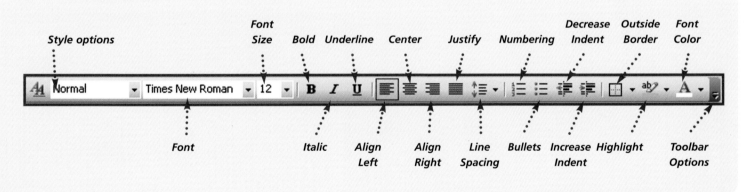

Style options · Font Size · Bold · Underline · Center · Justify · Numbering · Decrease Indent · Outside Border · Font Color

Font · Italic · Align Left · Align Right · Line Spacing · Bullets · Increase Indent · Highlight · Toolbar Options

Expert advice
You can create a new document via the Standard toolbar, or via the File menu. The File menu method gives you a choice of templates. You can select just a 'Blank Document' or you can choose from letters, faxes, reports, legal pleadings and so on. The Templates Wizard takes you step-by-step through procedures, such as writing a CV or creating an agenda.

Bright idea
If you make a mistake, just click the Undo button on the 'Standard' toolbar to rectify it. You can even go back in stages, until you get to a point where you were happy with your document.

Entering text

Type in your text and you will see it appear on the page of the open document. Unlike typing on a typewriter, you do not have to press the 'Return' key at the end of each line, as the text will automatically flow on to the next line. It doesn't matter if you make mistakes, as you can edit your work at any point, deleting text or moving it around the page.

SEE ALSO...

- **What is Word?** p 12
- **Explore the program** p 16
- **Spelling and grammar** p 58

BEFORE YOU START
*Open a document by going to the **File** menu and selecting **New**, then double- click the **Blank Document** icon. Alternatively, click the white **New Blank Document** icon on the toolbar.*

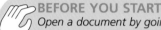

1 When you open a document or start a new document the cursor always appears at the very beginning of the first page. In Print Layout view, move the cursor to the point where you want to start typing. The pointer shape indicates how the text will be formatted, double click and then start typing your text.

2 In Word, text flows or 'wraps' automatically onto the next line when you reach the right-hand margin. You only need to press the Return key to start a new paragraph, or end a line early, or when making a list.

Click the **Show/Hide** button on the toolbar to reveal or hide non-printing characters, such as returns and spaces.

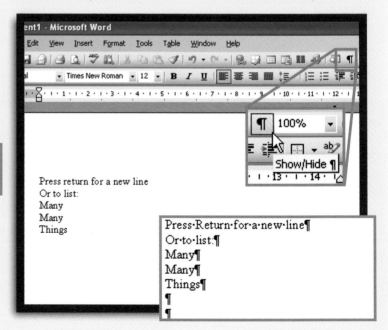

Expert advice

The keys on your computer's keyboard have different functions and different names. Some, such as the 'Shift' key, need to be held down while you press another key. Others, such as the 'Caps Lock' key, are known as toggle switches: press them once and they are switched on; press them again and they are switched off. The function keys (F1 to F12) are above the standard letter and number keys. These are used for keyboard commands.

Close up
Word can check spelling and grammar for you. A wavy red line appears under misspelt or unrecognisable words. Text that it thinks is grammatically incorrect is marked by a wavy green line.

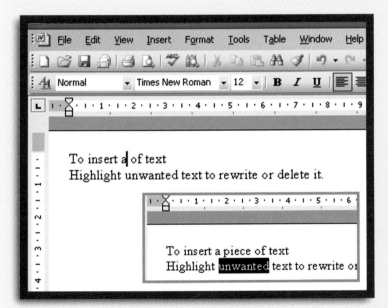

4 To type a capital letter, hold down the **Shift** key and press the letter key. Shift also causes the upper symbol on a key with two symbols, to be typed. For example, press **Shift + 5** to type '%'. If you want to type a series of capital letters, press the **Caps Lock** key. A green light on the right of your keyboard reminds you the lock is on. To unlock it, press **Caps Lock** once more.

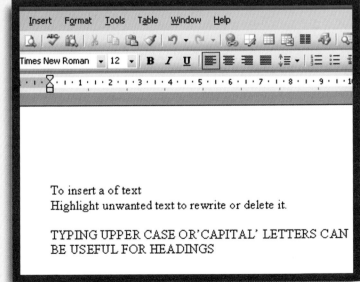

3 To insert words between existing text, move your cursor to the desired position, click and type. Use the **Backspace** key to delete errors to the left of the cursor. You can also delete text by clicking and dragging the mouse pointer over an area of text to highlight it, then pressing the **Backspace** or the **Delete** key. Or, you can highlight the text and type straight over it.

Save your work

Any new document should be saved as soon as possible after creating it, and you should continue to save any changes at regular intervals. This is important because sometimes computers crash, which means that your screen freezes and you have to exit the program without saving your files. So, if you don't save regularly, you run the risk of losing hours of work.

SEE ALSO...
- *Entering text* p 20
- *Import & export files* p 96
- *Create a Web site* p 98

BEFORE YOU START
To save a document for the first time, click on **File** in the Menu bar and choose **Save**. Alternatively, you can click the **Save** button on the toolbar, or use the keyboard shortcut **Ctrl + S**.

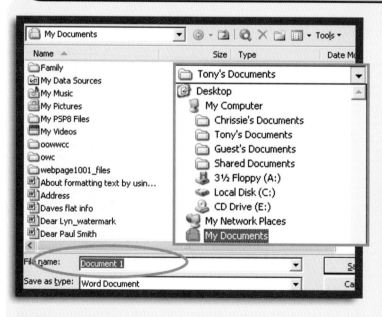

1 The first time you save a document, the 'Save As' dialogue box opens. You will need to name your document and choose where to save it. A suggested name, usually the first line, is highlighted in the 'File name' panel. Type a name over it.
   Word prompts you to save in the 'My Documents' folder. Click the arrow to the right of the panel if you want to choose a different location.

2 'My Documents' is a good place to store your work. However, it also makes sense to organise your files into subfolders – for instance, one folder for all your bank letters, another for your Web site, or a folder for each family member. If you want a new folder, click the **Create New Folder** icon and type in a name. To select and open the folder you wish to save into, double-click on it.

Expert advice
To save another version of a document go to the **File** menu and select **Save As**. You can then give the version a new name or choose to store it in an alternative location. This offers a quick and easy method for creating a backup file on floppy, Zip or Jaz disks, or for saving different versions of a file.

Bright idea
Create a template so you don't have to restyle your letters each time. Set up a page the way you want and save it. In the 'Save as type' panel, **select** *Document Template.* **Next time you create a new document, you can choose your template from the 'New' dialogue box.**

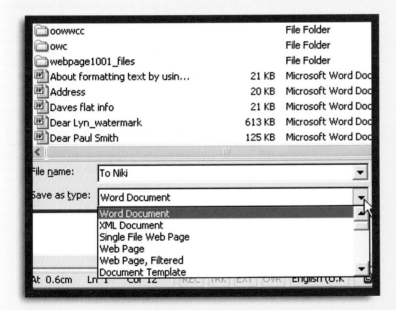

📁 oowwcc		File Folder
📁 owc		File Folder
📁 webpage1001_files		File Folder
📄 About formatting text by usin...	21 KB	Microsoft Word Doc
📄 Address	20 KB	Microsoft Word Doc
📄 Daves flat info	21 KB	Microsoft Word Doc
📄 Dear Lyn_watermark	613 KB	Microsoft Word Doc
📄 Dear Paul Smith	125 KB	Microsoft Word Doc

File name: To Niki

Save as type: Word Document

Word Document
XML Document
Single File Web Page
Web Page
Web Page, Filtered
Document Template

At 0.6cm   Ln 1   Col 12   REC TRK EXT OVR   English (U.K

4 When you are happy with your options, click the **Save** button. The file name in the blue Title bar at the top of the window changes from 'New document' to the name you have given it. As you work, you need to keep saving your changes. The quickest way is to click the 'floppy disk' icon on your toolbar, or press **Ctrl + S**.

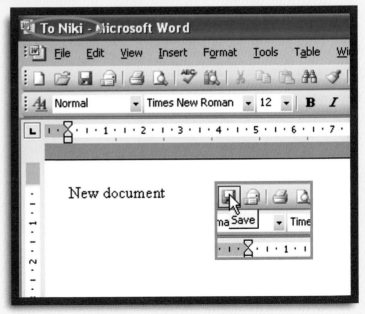

3 Choose how to save your file in the 'Save as type' panel. Most of the time you will save as a 'Word Document'. If you're creating a Web site, save your file as a 'Web Page'. 'Rich Text Format' retains your document setup, but can be opened by many other programs. 'Plain Text' saves files as text with no styling or formatting, but the text can then be read in almost any program.

Print your work

You are now ready to print out your pages. For the best results, take time to consider the appropriate layout for your document and to view how it will look before printing. Most printers allow you to vary the size of paper you use and to print envelopes and sticky labels. Depending on your printer, you may even be able to produce high quality photographic prints.

SEE ALSO...
- *Format documents* p 34
- *Headers and footers* p 52
- *Address labels* p 86

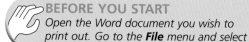

BEFORE YOU START
Open the Word document you wish to print out. Go to the **File** menu and select **Page Setup**. In the dialogue box, select the **Margins** tab. You can see how your page looks in the 'Preview' section.

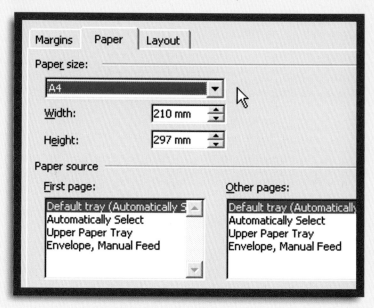

1 The margins are set to default values. To select a new value, click the up or down arrows beside each panel, or highlight the existing value and type a new number. Under 'Orientation', select **Portrait** (vertical) or **Landscape** (horizontal). See the difference between these two options in the 'Preview' section (top right).

2 Select the **Paper** tab, and check that the paper size is set to 'A4 210 x 297mm'. If it isn't, or you want a different paper size, click the down arrow and scroll down to choose the correct paper size.
If, for example, you want to print the first page of your document on pre-printed paper (like a letterhead), make your selections in the Paper source panel.

Look before you print

Before you print anything, it's a good idea to see what your document will look like. Go to the **File** menu and select **Print Preview**, or use the **Print Preview** button on the toolbar. The document is reduced so that the whole page fits the screen, enabling you to check that the layout is correct. To view several pages, select the **Multiple Pages** button on the Preview toolbar and drag across the number of pages you want. To enlarge the view, click on the page itself, or click on the down arrow beside the 'Zoom' button and choose a higher percentage.

4 Go to the **File** menu and click **Print**. Select your printer in the 'Name' panel. Under 'Page range', you can choose to print the whole document ('All'), the 'Current page', or a range of pages ('Pages'). To print a range, you will need to enter the page numbers. If you highlight an area of text in your document, you can click the 'Selection' button to print just that section.

3 Finally, click the **Layout** tab to change the position of the headers and footers in the 'From edge' section. Under Page 'Vertical alignment' you can choose how your text is positioned between the top and bottom margins of the page. Text is automatically aligned to the top. You can also number your lines and create borders for sections of text or whole pages. Click **OK** to finish.

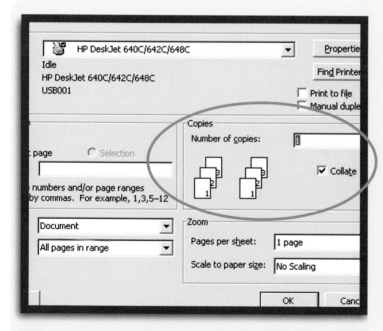

6 For double-sided printing, scroll down the options in the 'Print' panel and select **Odd pages**. Pages 1, 3, 5 and so on will then print. Once these are done, turn the printed sheets over, place them in your printer again and select **Even pages** in the 'Print' dialogue box. Click **OK** to print pages 2, 4, 6 and so on.

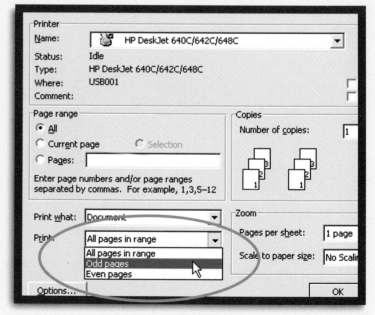

5 To print more than one copy of a document, click on the up arrow in the 'Number of copies' panel, or highlight the figure and type in the number of copies you want. Select the **Collate** option if you want your copies printed in page order within each set.

Styling Your Text

Choose and size a font

The appearance of any document can be changed dramatically through the use of different fonts, or 'typefaces', and by making text such as headings a different size. With a manual typewriter, you are limited to the keys on the machine. But with Word, you can use all sorts of different fonts and sizes, even on the same page.

SEE ALSO...
- *Style your text* p 30
- *Format documents* p 34

BEFORE YOU START
To change text to a different font, highlight the text that you want to change. You can then choose to make individual changes quickly, or to make several changes at once.

1 When you want to make several changes to your text – to alter font, size and style all at once, for example – it is quicker to do everything at the same time using the 'Font' dialogue box. Click on the **Format** menu and then on **Font** to open the dialogue box.

2 The default font for the template you are using is highlighted in the 'Font' panel. A line of your own text is shown in this default font in the 'Preview' panel at the bottom.

To see the text in a different font, scroll down the list in the 'Font' panel. Select a font name and look again in the 'Preview' pane to see your text displayed in the selected font.

3 Scroll through, select and view different typefaces (some of them have symbols, not letters). When you have chosen, click **OK** to confirm it. To change the default font for a template you are using, select a font and click on the **Default** button, then on **OK**. This changes the document and the template.

Serif or sans-serif

Two common fonts in use today are 'Times New Roman' and 'Arial'. 'Times New Roman' was developed as a typeface for *The Times* newspaper and is a serif font. This means that there are short, fine lines at the ends of the strokes of each character – this was thought to lead the eye smoothly from one letter to the next. 'Arial' was developed later, and is a sans-serif (without serif) font. Research has shown that a serif font is generally more readable when used in long documents, but that a sans-serif font is clearer for anyone who is partially sighted.

Times New Roman
Arial

Key word
The height of a font is measured in points, and there are precisely 72 points to an inch (2.5cm). A standard 12-point font measures one-sixth of an inch (4mm) in height on the page.

5 You can make individual changes to text more quickly by using the 'Formatting' toolbar. To alter the font, highlight your text and click on the down arrow to the right of the 'Font' panel. A drop-down list gives all the fonts available, with their names displayed in the associated typeface.

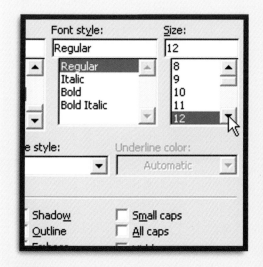

4 Using the arrows, scroll and select a font size from the list. If the size you want is not there, click on the box, type a figure, press **Return** and your text will change.

The largest standard font size is 72 point. If you need a bigger size, try using WordArt (see page 80). There are also various text effects to choose from, including shadows and embossed type.

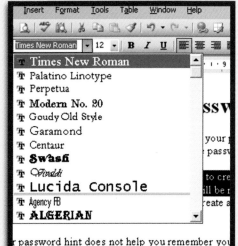

6 For quick changes to the size of an item of text, highlight it, then click on the down arrow to the right of the 'Font Size' box on the 'Formatting' toolbar. A drop-down menu lists point sizes. Click on one to select it.

Style and colour text

Changing the style of your text is a sure way to alter the look of a document and draw the reader's attention to specific points you wish to make. You can add emphasis and different styles to your characters by using specific enhancements, such as italics, or by underlining and colouring text. You can even use animated special effects to liven up your Web pages.

SEE ALSO...
- *Choose a font* p 28
- *Format paragraphs* p 36
- *Create a Web site* p 98

BEFORE YOU START
*Highlight the text you want to make changes to, click on the Format menu and select **Font**. By using this dialogue box, you can make several different changes to a piece of text.*

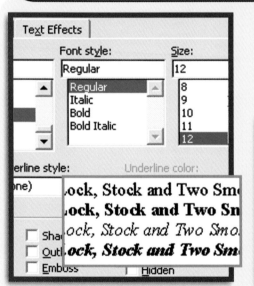

1 Select the style you wish to use in the 'Font style' panel. For emphasis, choose to embolden (Bold) or italicise (Italic) headings, rather than underlining them. Italicised text looks smaller than regular text, so you might want to embolden it, too. View changes in the 'Preview' pane.

2 To alter the colour of your selected text, click on the arrow by the 'Font color' panel. Select a colour by clicking on one of the square colour buttons. In the 'Preview' pane, you will see your coloured text.

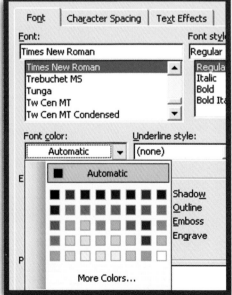

3 For a wider range of colours, click on **More Colors**. Select the **Standard** tab or the **Custom** tab for further choices. Click on a colour and it appears in the smaller 'New' pane.
Under the 'Custom' tab, you can customise the colour via the 'Color model' options for RGB (Red, Green, Blue) and HSL (Hue, Saturation, Luminesence). Click **OK** to finish.

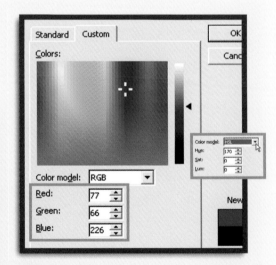

Watch out
Clicking on the 'Font Color' button, rather than on the arrow next to it, will change your text to the last colour chosen, instead of presenting you with a choice of colours.

Bright idea
'Hidden' text, which is one of the 'Effects' options, allows you to make notes in your document which will show on the computer screen but will not print out.

5 Click on the box of your choice in the 'Effects' section to select a further style. 'Superscript' is used for above-the-line text items like dates (16th), while 'Subscript' is for below-the-line items like 'H_2O'. Visual effects such as 'Emboss' and 'Engrave' can look faint in print depending on their colour.

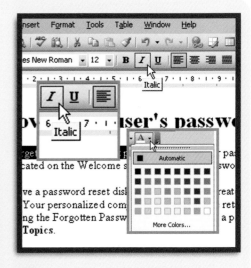

Strikethrough	If you forget your u
Double Strikethrough	If you forget your u
Superscript	If you ^{forget} your use
Subscript	If you $_{forget}$ your use
Shadow	If you forget your u
Outline	If you forget your u
Emboss	If you forget your u
Engrave	If you forget your u
Small Caps	IF YOU FORGET YO
All Caps	IF YOU FORGET
Hidden	

4 Click on the arrow beside 'Underline style' for a drop-down menu of line styles. Use the scroll bar to move up and down. Click on a style to select it, then click on the arrow beside 'Underline color' to select a colour for the line.

6 If you want to use only one of these functions, it is quicker to use the shortcut icons on the 'Formatting' toolbar. You can change the font colour, as well as embolden, italicise and underline selected text. However, these buttons have limited functions. For example, you cannot underline in colour, nor access the 11 additional 'Effects' in the 'Font' dialogue box.

8 Imagine you have typed a heading, or your address, at the top of a page or column. You have centred the text, but the letters look too tightly squeezed together – you want to stretch them across without altering the font size. Click on the 'Spacing' panel, select **Expanded** and use the 'By' panel to define an amount. Select **Condensed** for the opposite effect.

7 In the 'Font' dialogue box, click on the **Character Spacing** tab. If you have different font sizes within your selected text, and you want to scale the size of the text up or down without altering the font sizes, click the 'Scale' panel and select a percentage.

9 Click on the **Text Effects** tab. Select an animated effect from the list in the 'Animations' panel, view what it does to your text in the 'Preview' pane. Click **OK** to confirm your choice and return to your document.

Styling Your Document

Format a document

The overall appearance of a document is determined by the formatting characteristics set up within the template in which you open it. You may want to add a new heading or items, such as page numbers. If a pre-set heading is not quite perfect, you can modify it. If you work on many documents of the same type, you may even want to create your own style and save it as a template.

SEE ALSO...
- *Choose a font* p 28
- *Format paragraphs* p 36
- *AutoFormat* p 46

BEFORE YOU START
Templates for document formats are sub-divided into various styled paragraph and character items. If you are happy with the style options in the template, use AutoFormat (See p.46).

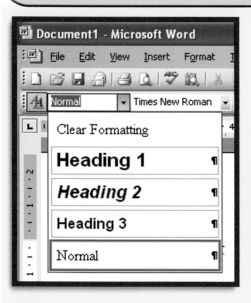

1 Highlight your text. Click on the down arrow in the 'Style' panel on the 'Formatting' toolbar. A drop-down list displays styles available to the current document.

Click on a style to apply to the selected text. Select **Normal** or **Clear formatting** to remove styling.

2 Go to the **Format** menu and click on **Styles and Formatting** to open the Task Pane listing more pre-set styles. Hover the pointer over a style to check its details, if you're happy click to select it.

Click on the arrow on the right of the 'Show' panel, to view various styles and formatting options. For example, choose 'All styles' to view all available formatting styles.

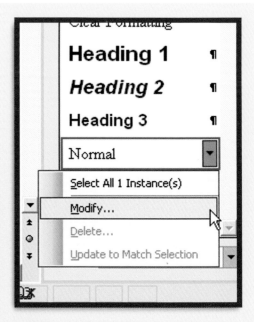

3 Styles are defined as either ('¶') paragraph, or ('a') character, to show whether they apply to a paragraph or line.

To alter a style, select it in the 'Styles and Formatting' task pane and click on the **Modify** option.

Themes

You can style text using themes to supply an integrated look for your document, including fonts, colours and related graphics, such as 'bullets'. Go to the **Format** menu and select **Themes**. Although fine for designing Web pages and on-screen documents, be aware that the background will not print. Deselect the 'Background image' box to view how the theme would look if you wanted to print the page.

Watch out

If you save changes to the original template, you can end up with a whole mixture of muddled styles. It is better to save new or modified styles as a new template, giving it a name you will recognise. To do this, go to the **File** menu, click **Save As** and select **Document Template** in the 'Save as type' panel.

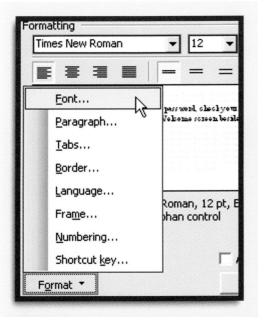

4 Click on the **Format** button to access a drop-down menu. Select and change any style details by clicking on each heading to open the appropriate dialogue box.
You can change the font and size, paragraphing, indents and so on.

5 Select **Add to template** only if you wish to use the modified style in new documents based on the same template. Select **Automatically update** to update all previous instances of that style in your document. Click on **OK** to modify the formatting for the selected paragraph and to return to the document. The modified style is now available on the 'Formatting' toolbar.

6 Select the **New Style** button in the 'Styles and Formatting' task pane to create a new style. Name it and modify items, selecting and defining those you need. You can add to the list at any time. Use the new styles and, when finished, save a version of your document to be used as a template for other documents of the same kind.

Format a paragraph

Just as you can easily change the look of your entire document, so you can also change the layout, or 'format', of individual sections within it. Quoted text can be indented, either from the left or from both sides, while hanging indents can give a traditional look to your work. You can also prevent a single line straying on to the next page, or being left behind.

SEE ALSO...
- *Format documents* p 34
- *Using tabs* p 40
- *AutoFormat* p 46

BEFORE YOU START
*Highlight several paragraphs or click anywhere in a single paragraph to select it. Click on the **Format** menu and select **Paragraph**. Then click on the **Indents and Spacing** tab.*

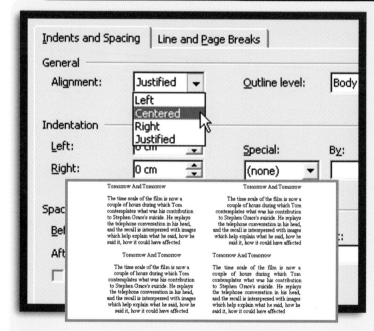

1 In the 'Alignment' panel, **Left** is already selected by default, so your text is lined up to the left side of the page. Click on the arrow to the right to centre text on the page (Centered), to make it line up to the right side of the page (Right), or to stretch and align the text so that it is straight on both sides (Justified).

2 Under 'Indentation', select the 'Right' or 'Left' panel and scroll to select how far in from the left or right edge of the page you want to set the text. This is good for indenting quotes.

Click in the 'Special' panel and select **First line**. Click **By** to determine how far in from the main body of the paragraph the first line will be set. Select **Hanging** to indent all lines in a paragraph except for the first.

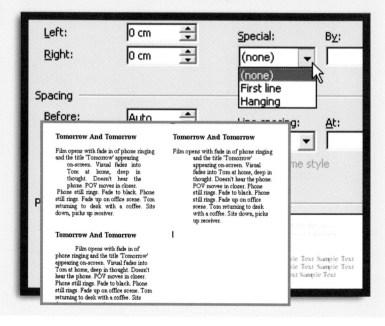

Toolbar shortcuts

You can also set the alignment by clicking on the alignment buttons on the Formatting toolbar.

Paragraph indents can be changed by using the small 'Indent' markers at either end of the ruler at the top of the screen. Let your mouse hover over them. 'ScreenTips' show four types on the left: 'First Line'; 'Left Margin'; 'Hanging Indent'; and 'Left Indent'.

Hanging Indent

Bright idea
To change from single to double line spacing quickly, highlight the text, hold down the Ctrl key and press the number 2 on the keyboard. To return to single line spacing, hold down the Ctrl key and press 1.

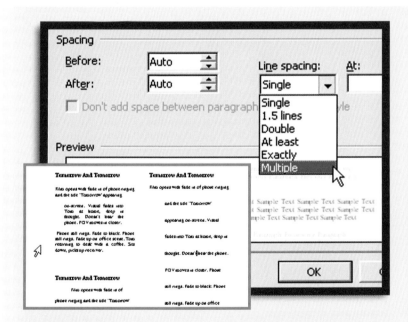

4 Click on the **Line and Page Breaks** tab. The default 'Widow and Orphan' controls stop the last line of a paragraph appearing by itself at the top of the following page, or the first line being left on its own at the bottom of the previous page. You can fine-tune paragraph breaks, and opt to remove line numbers, or to turn off automatic hyphenation of words.

3 Select the 'Before' and 'After' panels to specify how much space will run before and after paragraphs in the selected text. Click in the 'Line spacing' panel to alter the spacing between lines within the paragraph. Letters are usually 'single' spaced, while typing draft documents in 'double spacing' leaves room for corrections. You can also set an exact amount of space or multiple lines.

Using columns and bullets

One very effective way of changing the appearance of your document is to put your text in columns. Try this with documents such as newsletters as it makes large amounts of text much easier to read. Alternatively, adding bullet points will help to display lists in a more accessible and logical way, while improving the overall look of your document.

SEE ALSO...
- *Format documents* p 34
- *Using tabs* p 40
- *Using tables* p 48

BEFORE YOU START
Although you can format text into columns after you have finished typing, it is sensible to set the number of columns first, so you have a rough idea of how your pages will look.

1 In the **Format** menu, click on **Columns**. In the dialogue box, select the number of columns you require, either by choosing one of the pre-set options or by typing the number into the appropriate panel. Then, either tick the 'Equal column width' box for evenly spaced columns, or specify the width of each column individually.

2 Your column format will apply to the whole of the document, unless you specify otherwise. If, for example, you need a heading, enter this first, leave a few line spaces and then set up your column format. In the dialogue box, make sure you have selected **This point forward** in the 'Apply to' panel.

The final formatting option allows you to put a visible line between your columns. Click **OK** when your formatting is complete.

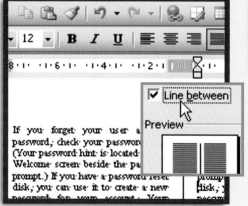

3 The cursor appears in your first column for you to begin typing. When the first column is full, your text will run straight into the next one. To force text over into the next column, position your cursor where you want the break, go to the **Insert** menu, select **Break**, and then click **Column break**.

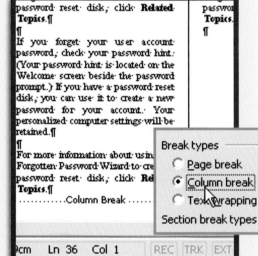

Use your ruler

Column width can be altered quickly using the ruler at the top of the page. Grey areas relate to margins between the columns. Click the edge of a column and drag it to the required size. If you select equal column width, all columns will alter to match. You can change page margins in the same way.

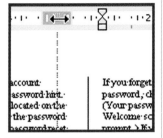

Bright idea

Use the 'Columns' button on the 'Formatting' toolbar as a quick-click method of putting the text in your document into columns.

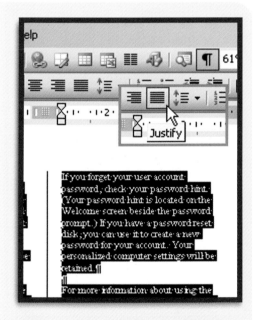

4 Your text can then be styled and formatted in the normal way. To avoid awkward line ends in narrow columns, it is a good idea to justify your text. This will give it a more professional look. Highlight the text and click on the **Justify** icon on the 'Formatting' toolbar.

1 To give your text added emphasis, use bullet points. In the **Format** menu, click on **Bullets and Numbering**. The dialogue box that appears gives you a range of bullet point styles or numbers to choose from. Click on the appropriate tab and select a style of bullet. Click **OK**. Each time you press 'Return' in your text, a new bullet or number will be added.

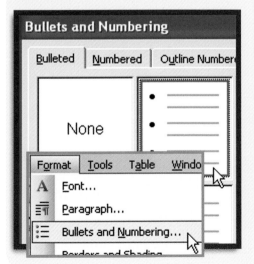

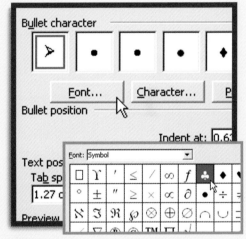

2 From the 'Bullets and Numbering' dialogue box you can also alter the appearance of your bullets. Click on **Customize** then **Font** to alter the size and font. Click on **Character** to view a whole range of character options. Select a character, then click **OK**. The 'Bullet position' and 'Text position' sections let you determine how far to indent your bullets, numbers or text. Check the 'Preview' pane for the result.

Using tabs

The 'Tab' feature allows you to align your text – or 'tabulate' it. This is a quick way of moving words across the page, rather than pressing the spacebar repeatedly. While you would create a table to organise lots of information into columns and rows, tabs are a handy way of tidying up a letter, an invoice, or a few simple columns of information.

SEE ALSO...
- *Using columns* p 38
- *Using tables* p 48
- *Sort a list* p 92

BEFORE YOU START
When you are working with tabs, it is a good idea to have the tabs *showing. Click on the Show/Hide button in the toolbar to reveal them, if they are not already visible.*

1 Microsoft Word opens with tabs set at the default position of 0.5 inches or metric equivalent. Pressing the **Tab** key on your keyboard causes the cursor to jump along the line to these preset positions.

2 If you need to set your own tabs instead of using the default ones, highlight the document or the section to which tabs should apply. Go to the **Format** menu and click **Tabs**.
Enter the position of your first tab in the 'Tab stop position' panel, using the ruler at the top of the page as a guide. Add as many tabs as you need, clicking **Set** after each one.

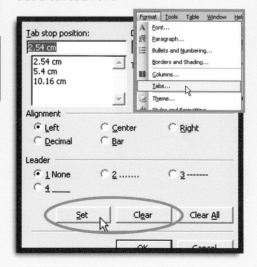

3 The 'Tabs' dialogue box gives you further options, including changing the alignment of your tabs. The default setting is aligned to the left, but you can align the tabs to the middle ('Center') of the text or to the right.

Tab shortcut

A quick way to set your tabs is by using the ruler at the top of the page. Highlight your text. Then, simply by clicking on the ruler at the required tab position, a left-aligned tab will be set. To change the alignment, click on the top left-hand corner to change the icon from left- to centre- or right-aligned tabs.

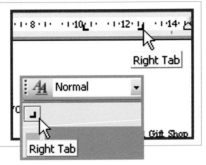

5 A further option allows you to fill in the space between your tabs with a type of line called a leader. The default setting is 'none', but you can click on the appropriate radio button beneath **Leader** to select dots, a broken line or a solid line. These options work especially well when you are displaying columns of figures.

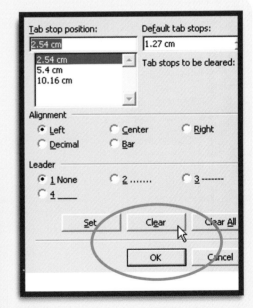

4 If your tabulated text includes figures, select the **Decimal** alignment button. This aligns all your numbers at the decimal point. Selecting **Bar** gives you a vertical dividing line at the position of the tab.

6 The bottom of the Tabs dialogue box has a number of buttons. To delete a tab you've set, select it and click **Clear**. Click **Clear All** to automatically remove all of your tabs.
    When you're happy with your settings, click **OK** to return to your document.

Design a letterhead

Using a personalised letterhead will add a touch of flair and individuality to all your correspondence. Once you've created one letterhead, you can follow the same principles to design letterheads for different circumstances – one for business stationery, perhaps. Save your letterhead as a template and you can use it whenever you write a letter.

SEE ALSO...
- **Choose a font** p 28
- **Format documents** p 34
- **Headers and footers** p 52

BEFORE YOU START
Open up a new document, go to the **File** menu and click on **Page Setup**.

Click on the **Layout** tab, set the margins and in the 'From edge' section, set the Header figure. Click **OK**.

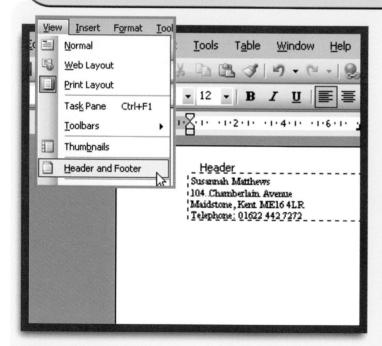

1 A good way to create your letterhead is within the 'Header' section of your document. Go to the **View** menu and click on **Header and Footer**. The cursor automatically appears in the 'Header' section. Type in your name, address and telephone number.

2 Highlight your name, go to the **Format** menu and click on the **Font** tab. Scroll through the list of Fonts and select one. Choose a style and size, clicking on any to view them in the Preview window. Click **OK**. Now style your address in the same way.

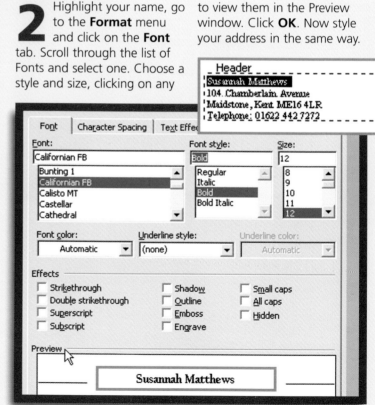

Key word

The terms header and footer describe the information that appears at the top (header) and bottom (footer) of each page of a document – for example, running titles, reference details and page numbers.

Line spacing

The 'Format/Paragraph' dialogue box allows you to adjust line spacing between larger sections of highlighted text. Click on the arrow beside the 'Line spacing' panel, then click on a suitable measurement. Click **OK**.

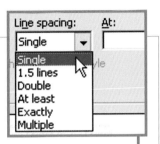

4 You can adjust the spacing above or below your lines. Select some or all of your header text and go to **Format** then **Paragraph**. In the 'Spacing' section, click on the arrows beside 'Before' or 'After' to adjust the increment.

Check the 'Preview' panel to see what your changes will look like. Click **OK**.

3 To position your letterhead in the centre of the page, highlight all of the text in your Header section, go to the **Format** menu and choose **Paragraph**. Click on the black arrow next to the 'Alignment' panel (right), and select **Centered** from the drop-down menu. Click **OK**.

Use your toolbar
The toolbar buttons at the top of the screen help you to style your text quickly. Highlight the text. Click on the relevant button to make it bold, to italicise it or to underline it. Change the position of your text, too, by clicking on the 'Left', 'Centre', 'Right' or 'Justify' alignment buttons.

Bright idea
Save time and effort by using Word's automatic dating facility for your letters. Click where you want the date to appear in your document, go to the **Insert** menu and select **Date and Time**. In the dialogue box choose your preferred style and click **OK**.

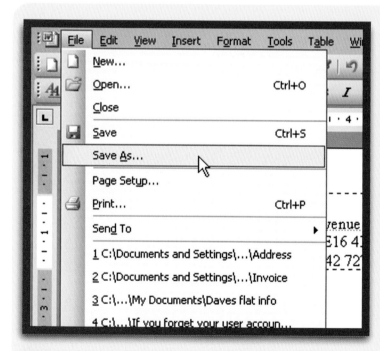

6 In the 'Save As' dialogue box you will see from the 'Save in' panel that Word, by default, suggests saving your document in its 'Templates' folder. Type in a suitable name for your template in the 'File name' panel, and then click on the **Save** button.

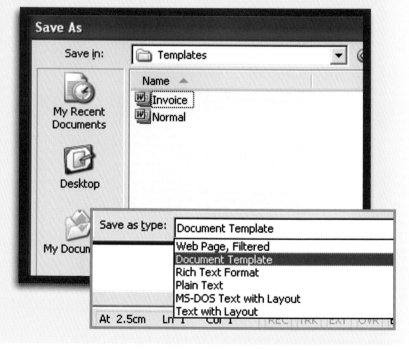

5 When you are happy with your design, save it as a template so that you can use it repeatedly. Go to the **File** menu and select **Save As**. Scroll through the 'Save as type' drop-down menu at the bottom of the dialogue box and select **Document Template**.

Let the Wizard help

Microsoft Word has useful wizards that help you create personalised letterheads. Open Word, go to the **File** menu and click **New**. The 'New Document' task pane displays your options. Under Templates, select 'On my computer'. Select the **Letters & Faxes** tab and choose a style.

The wizard will guide you through the process. You can then save your completed document as a template for future use.

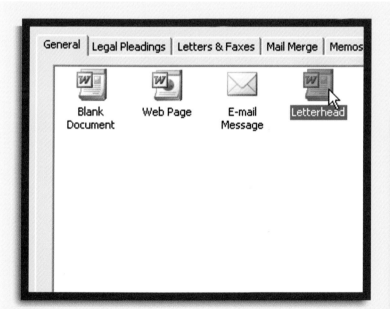

7 Whenever you want to use your template to write a letter, simply open Word, go to the **File** menu and click on **New**. The 'New Document' task pane will display your options. Under the Templates section, select 'On my computer'. Your template will appear under the 'General' tab. Click on the icon for your letterhead to open up the template. Then click **OK**.

8 When the template opens, go to the **File** menu and click **Save As**. Select a folder in which to save your letter, type in a name for it, then click on **Save**. The cursor will flash below your letterhead. Press the **Return** key about five times, then start typing.

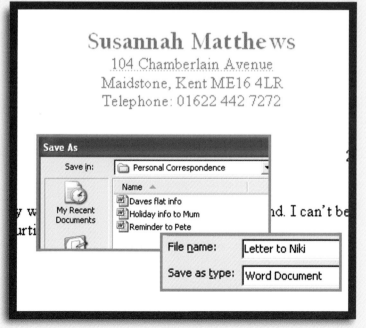

AutoFormat your text

The AutoFormat feature applies standard headings and text styles to your documents, giving them a professional finish. You can choose exactly how to format your text and then either have your work formatted automatically as you type, or format a whole document when you have completed it. Word enables you to review and accept or reject the changes.

SEE ALSO...
- *Format documents* p 34
- *Wizards & templates* p 50
- *AutoCorrect* p 62

CHOOSE YOUR STYLE
Whether you are typing a letter, an e-mail or a fax, Word can style your page for you.

Formatting text as you type
To format your text automatically as you type, you need to tell Word what you want it to change. Go to the **Tools** menu and choose

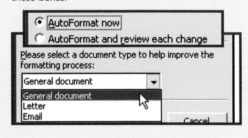

AutoCorrect Options. Select the **AutoFormat As You Type** tab and select the options you require. If you want to wait until you have finished before using AutoFormat, untick all of these boxes.

Formatting an existing document
When you have finished typing and are ready to format your document, go to the **Format** menu and select **AutoFormat**.

If you want Word to do this without input from you, select **AutoFormat now**. Otherwise, click **AutoFormat and review each change** so

that you can approve changes. Unless instructed, Word formats text as a general document. If you want a letter or an e-mail format, click on the drop-down menu beneath 'Please select a document type…' and choose from the list.

Click on **Options** for preferred settings, which are mostly the same as those on the 'AutoFormat As You Type' tab. However, a few options at the top and bottom of the dialogue boxes differ.

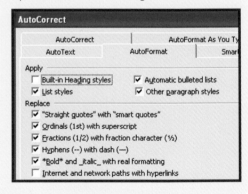

Close up
If you're AutoFormatting a list as you type it, you'll need to tell Word when you've finished the list. To do this, either press the Return key twice, or press it once and then press the Backspace key once.

Close up
For more information on the various AutoFormat options, right-click on an option then left-click on What's This? in the pop-up menu.

Some of your AutoFormat options

Built-in Headings Select this option when Word

formats a completed document, but leave it unticked when Word formats as you type, as it is easier to apply heading styles when you have an overview of the whole document.

List styles Tick this box if you want to apply the standard style for bulleted and numbered lists. Word removes any bullets or numbers that you've inserted and replaces them with preset styles. Select the **Styles** box in the 'Preserve' section to retain any styles you previously applied to your document,

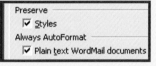

when you run AutoFormat. This option is only available for styling completed documents. Choose your options, then click **OK** and **OK** again. After a few seconds, your page is reformatted, and the AutoFormat dialogue box appears.

Reviewing changes

If you like the way the document looks, click **Accept All**. If you don't like it, click **Reject All**.

Alternatively, you can go through the entire document, accepting and rejecting each formatting change. Click **Review Changes**. Your text reappears with blue and red 'invisibles', indicating formatting changes that have been made. An explanation of each change is given in the dialogue box.

Accepting or rejecting changes

If you're happy with a formatting change, click the ⇨ **Find** button to accept it and jump to the next change. If you don't like a change, click the **Reject** button to undo it. If you reject a change and then decide to keep it after all, click the **Undo** button on the 'Formatting' toolbar.

To see what the document looks like without the distracting revision marks, select the **Hide Marks** button. When you've finished reviewing the changes, click **Cancel**. To apply the formats you've accepted, click the **Accept All** button in the 'AutoFormat' dialogue box.

Choosing a different look

If you want to change the appearance of your document completely, go to the **Format** menu and select **AutoFormat**. Make sure the **Auto Format and review each change** button is

selected and click **OK**. Now click the **Style Gallery** button (see left).

All the document templates are displayed in the left pane. Click on a template and then select 'Preview' **Document** to update the 'Preview of' pane on the right.

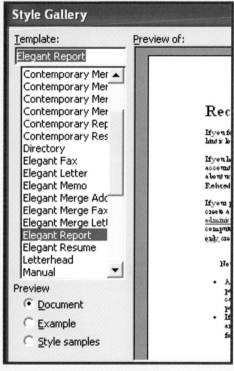

Alternatively, select **Example** in the 'Preview' section, to preview a sample document. When you have found a template that suits your needs, click **OK**, and then close the dialogue box.

Bright idea
If you are unhappy with the way that AutoFormat has changed your pages, press the Undo *button on the 'Formatting' toolbar or choose* Undo *from the* Edit *menu.*

Key word
Invisibles are the symbols used to represent specific instances of formatting in a document, such as a paragraph break, indent or tab. They are only for visual reference on screen, and do not print with the rest of your document.

Using tables

Tables provide an ideal structure for organising and presenting information. Table data can be sorted alphabetically, numerically, or by date, and you can treat the table like a mini-spreadsheet and use it to perform calculations. Word 2000 also lets you move the table around the page, or position it exactly where you want within text.

SEE ALSO...
- *Using columns* p 38
- *Using tabs* p 40
- *Wizards & templates* p 50

BEFORE YOU START
Think about how many columns and rows you are likely to need – a rough sketch might help you to decide. Extra rows are easy to add, but new columns require a little more sorting out.

1 In the **Table** menu, click on **Insert** then **Table** and select the required number of columns and rows in the dialogue box. 'Fixed column width' spreads columns out evenly across the page. 'AutoFit to contents' widens columns to fit typed text or graphics, while 'AutoFit to window' allows the table to fit a Web browser window.

2 Click the **Autoformat** button to choose one of the preset 'Table AutoFormat' options. The list of 'Table styles' gives you a number of choices, together with a preview below.
Further formatting choices can be made by ticking or unticking the boxes provided. Check the preview pane to see the effect your choices make and click **OK** to confirm. Click **OK** again, to close the 'Insert Table' dialogue box.

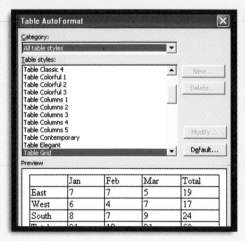

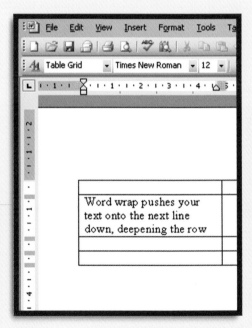

3 Type in your text. To move from cell to cell, press the **Tab** key, or use your mouse to position your cursor. You can type any amount of text in a cell, as the size of all the cells in that row will increase to accommodate it.

Formatting your table

To customise your table, select **Table Properties** from the **Table** menu. From here, you can alter the position of your table on the page and the way text wraps around it. Clicking on the **Borders and Shading** button allows you to alter the appearance of each cell and to show or hide as much of the grid as needed.

Watch out

When you draw a table, you need to choose the style, colour and line width before you begin to draw. It can be quicker to insert a table and adjust the formatting later.

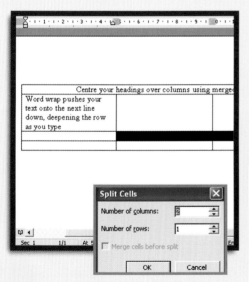

4 To merge cells together – so you can type a heading, for example – click and drag your mouse over the cells to select them. Go to the **Table** menu and select **Merge Cells**. To split cells, to create more than originally specified, highlight the row, click the **Table** menu, select **Split Cells** and change the number of columns. Click **OK**.

5 For a more complex, customised table, click on the **Table** menu and choose **Draw Table**. Your cursor changes to a pencil shape and the 'Tables and Borders' toolbar appears. You can use this toolbar to change the line width, colour and style of your table. To draw a red table for example, click on the **Pencil** button and select red in the drop-down menu.

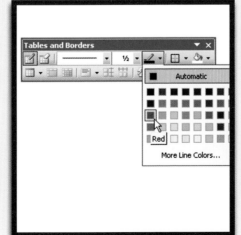

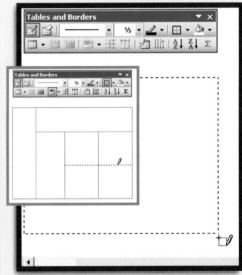

6 Create the outline of the table by clicking on the page and dragging the pencil diagonally until the table is the size you want. Draw in the row and column lines by dragging the pencil cursor from one edge of the box to the other. Then close the toolbar to enter your text.

Wizards and templates

Every time you create a new document, you are offered the 'Blank Document' template, which is an empty document with a pre-defined layout. However, there are a variety of other templates available, some of which are also wizards. These lead you step by step through common procedures, such as creating your curriculum vitae or a fax.

SEE ALSO...
- *Design a letterhead* p 42
- *Make address labels* p 86
- *Create a Web site* p 98

 BEFORE YOU START
*From the **File** menu select **New**. This opens the 'New Document' Task Pane.*

Under 'Templates' click 'On my computer'. The 'Templates' dialogue box has eight template wizard tabs.

2 The template tells you where to enter your details. To replace this text, just highlight it and type in your details – for example, highlight the heading 'Company Name Here', then type in your own company name. Where instructions are given in square brackets, just click inside them to highlight the words and then type in your own text.

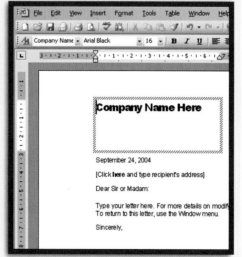

1 To use a letter template, click on the **Letters & Faxes** tab. Select one of the three letter styles – 'Elegant', 'Professional' or 'Contemporary'. View the style in the 'Preview' pane on the right. Select the one you want, and click **OK**.

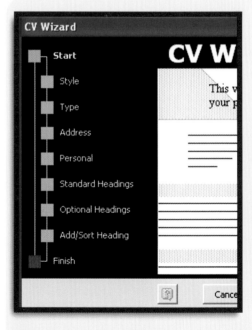

1 To use a wizard to make a CV, or résumé, for example, click on the **Other Documents** tab, select **Resume Wizard** and click **OK**. On the left is a list of the various stages. Green indicates where you are. Click **Next**.

That's amazing!
You can create your own templates to re-use as often as you wish. To save a document as a template, click on **File**, then **Save As**. Name your file. In the 'Save as type' panel, select **Document Template**. Your new template will be added to the other templates available when you create a new document.

Watch out
Many of the templates provided by Word were created specifically for American users. This means that they may not always be appropriate in the UK.

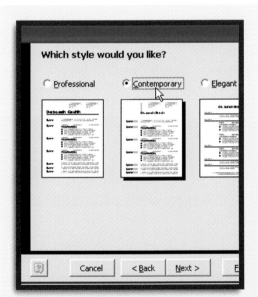

3 Select the personal items you would like in your CV from a list of options. The next window offers standard options for section headings while the following one has specialised options. Click **Next**. You can also type any heading that has not so far been on offer, and edit those already selected.

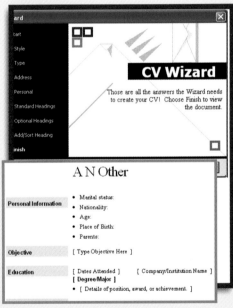

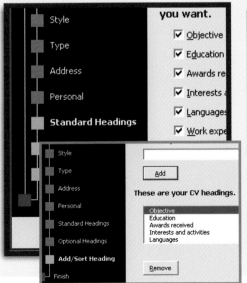

2 Select which style you want by clicking the appropriate radio button. Click **Next**. You will then be asked about the type of CV you want to create. Choose from the options then click **Next**. Click in the relevant boxes in the following window, typing in your name and other details. Click **Next.**

4 When you reach the end of the wizard, click on the **Finish** button. Your customised document template opens with your selected headings, ready to receive your details. You can now start to type them in.

Headers and footers

Headers and footers enable you to add running information to your pages, such as page numbers. They appear in the top or bottom margins of your document, outside the normal print area. Anything that you insert in a header or footer appears on every page of your document, unless you specify otherwise.

BEFORE YOU START
*To add a header or footer to a document, click on the **View** menu and choose **Header and Footer**. A toolbar appears that allows you to enter text and style it as you wish.*

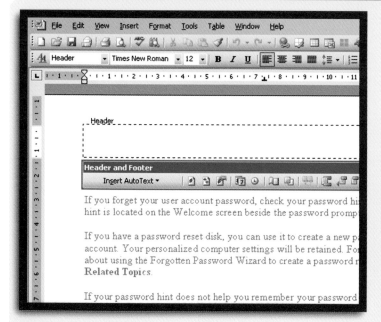

2 You can align your header text to the left, centre or right using the toolbar buttons (below). Press the **Tab** key to move along the box and type in your header text. To move from the header to the footer, click on the **Switch Between Header and Footer** button on the toolbar. Type your text into the footer as appropriate.

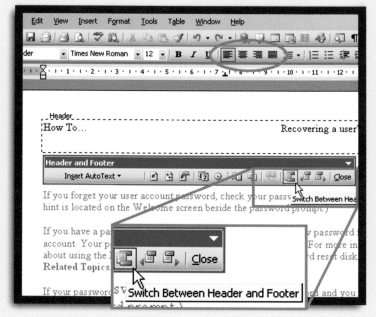

1 Once you have the 'Header and Footer' toolbar on screen, you will notice that your cursor is flashing on the left of the header, ready for you to enter text or an image. You will also notice that the text in the main body of your document looks faint, meaning that it is not accessible or editable while you are in this view.

Using the toolbar

You'll find lots of useful features in the 'Header and Footer' toolbar: Use 'Insert Date' and 'Insert Time' to show when you created a document. Use 'Page Setup' to set your options, such as having different headers and footers on odd and even pages.

Use 'Show Previous' and 'Show Next' to jump between headers or footers.

By default, headers and footers are identical on every page. If you want different footers on each page, jump to your next footer and click the **Link to Previous** button to deselect it. Now type your text.

Watch out

If you just type in your page number in a header or footer, this same number will be repeated on every page. Click and use the Insert Page Number *button instead (see Step 3).*

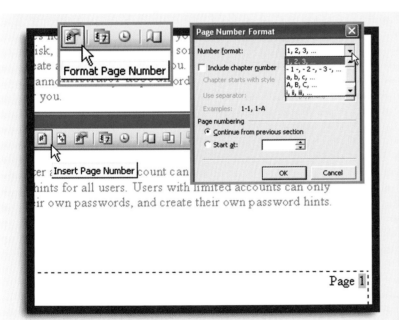

Page Number Format

Number format: 1, 2, 3, …

☐ Include chapter number

Chapter starts with style

Use separator:

Examples: 1-1, 1-A

Page numbering
◉ Continue from previous section
○ Start at:

OK   Cancel

---

4 You can style the header and footer as you would any text. Click the formatting buttons to increase the font size or to make it bold or italic. You can also add a border. Highlight your header or footer, go to the **Format** menu and choose **Borders and Shading**. Select a line style, then click the appropriate border in the 'Preview' pane. Click **OK**, then **Close** to return to your text.

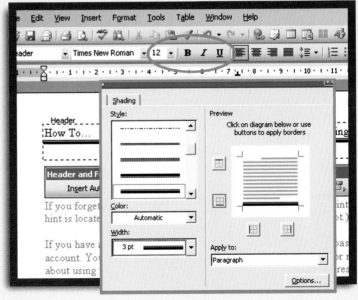

3 To add a page number, position your cursor where you want it to appear in your footer and click on the **Insert Page Number** icon on the Header and Footer toolbar. Style the page number by clicking on the **Format Page Number** icon.

In the dialogue box, select a format from the drop-down menu. Choose what number to start the pages with under 'Page numbering'. Click **OK**.

Inserting text breaks

Sometimes you'll want to start a new page, column or section before you have filled the last one with text. You might do this by pressing the 'Return key' repeatedly, but Word has a quicker way of creating breaks in text. You'll also have more control over the look and shape of your work, as you can reformat the text in each section to make it easier to read.

SEE ALSO...
- *Format documents* p 34
- *Using columns* p 38

BREAKING UP TEXT

To break your text in a particular place, you need to insert a permanent break, which will remain unaffected by Word's automatic pagination.

Position the cursor in your document where you wish to make the break. You can create a break before you type any more text, or you can add

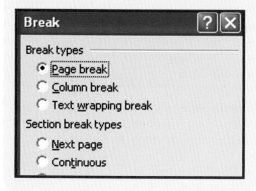

breaks after you've typed your document. Go to the **Insert** menu and select **Break** to open the dialogue box.

Break types

To move text onto a new page, select the **Page break** radio button. No matter how you alter the document, this text will always start at the top of a new page.

If you want a column to end before it reaches the bottom of the page, select **Column break**.

Finally, select the **Text wrapping break** option to force text to the beginning of a new line.

Section break types

If you want to format a part of your document differently on a separate page, select the section break option **Next page**. Now you can set text on that page over a different number of columns, or make it landscape (horizontal) while the rest of your document is portrait (vertical). If you want to incorporate a different layout within the same page, select **Continuous**.

If you have created a document with facing pages, like a book, choose **Odd page** or **Even page** to start a new section on the next odd- or even-numbered page.

Deleting breaks

If you no longer want a break, double-click the break to select it, then press the **Delete** key. You can also position your cursor after the break and press **Backspace**. If you can't see the dotted line break on your screen, click the **Show/Hide** button on the Standard toolbar.

Bright idea
A quick way to insert a Page break is to hold down the Ctrl *key and press the* Return *key.*

Watch out
It is best not to create a page break by pressing the 'Return' key continuously until you reach a new page. Your text is fluid and will move up or down as you add or delete text later. The result is much more time consuming than using Word's built-in Break feature.

Editing Text

Cut, copy and paste

Word enables you to reorganise a document in no time by taking text, or images, from one area and placing them in another – this is called 'cutting and pasting'. If text needs to be repeated, you can copy it, leaving the original intact. You can then paste the text as many times as you like, wherever you like, without the need to type it all again.

SEE ALSO...
- *Wizards & Templates* p 50
- *Add a picture* p 74

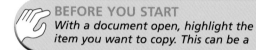

BEFORE YOU START
With a document open, highlight the item you want to copy. This can be a word, a phrase, a paragraph, a whole page, even several pages, or an illustration, such as a piece of ClipArt.

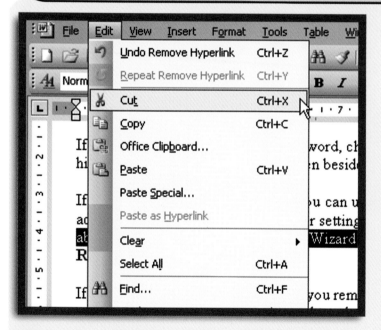

1 Go to the **Edit** menu and select either **Cut** or **Copy**. Text is stored on the computer's Clipboard, waiting to be used. If you are unsure of the effect of any changes, use 'Copy' then go back and delete unwanted text after pasting. Left-click in the document so that the insertion point appears where you want to paste the text.

2 Go to the **Edit** menu and click **Paste**. Your text appears in the new location. You may need to check and readjust the spacing in your document. To move text just a short distance, highlight it, then drag and drop it on the page wherever you wish.

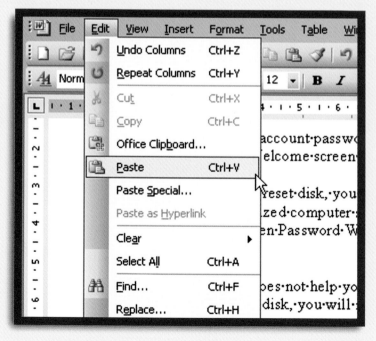

Shortcuts
The 'Cut', 'Copy', and 'Paste' buttons on the 'Formatting' toolbar offer a speedy way to reorganise your work. Keyboard shortcuts for these commands, shown on the 'Edit' menu, are, respectively, **Ctrl + X**, **Ctrl + C** and **Ctrl + V**. If you inadvertently give a keyboard command, rather than typing in, say, a capital 'V', remember to click on the **Undo** button immediately to correct the mistake.

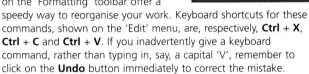

Key word
Cut and paste get their names from the publishing procedures used many years ago. Long strips of text called 'galleys' were actually cut up and then pasted on to blank page layouts.

4 You can also use the 'Copy' and 'Paste' commands to move text or images between two open Word documents. You can use the 'Paste Special' command on the 'Edit' menu to copy text on to the clipboard – from there, you can transfer text or images to other programs or to a Web page, in the appropriate format.

3 The clipboard stores up to 24 items at any time, depending on their size. With the insertion point at the correct position in the text, click on **Edit** and select **Office Clipboard**. The Clipboard task bar appears in the Task Pane and displays your cut and copied items as thumbnails. Click on the arrow next to the item you wish to 'Paste' then click **Paste**. If you want to remove the item click **Delete**.

Spelling and grammar

Word can check both spelling and grammar on screen as you type, enabling you to correct your mistakes immediately. If you prefer to check your work once you've finished typing, you can switch these features off and run a single check on the whole document. You can also create your own custom dictionaries to include special words.

SEE ALSO...
● *Thesaurus* p 60
● *AutoCorrect* p 62
● *Change your preferences* p 66

BEFORE YOU START
Go to the **Tools** menu, click on **Language** and **Set Language**.

In the dialogue box, select the language you wish to use. Remember that UK and US English are different.

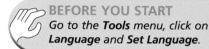

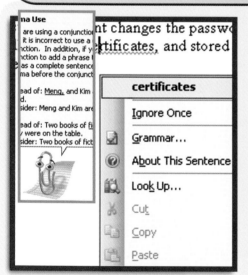

certificates

Ignore Once

Grammar...

About This Sentence

Look Up...

Cut

Copy

Paste

1 As you type, Word automatically checks your spelling and grammar. Right-click on a word marked with a wavy underline to select an alternative word from the pop-up menu.

If you don't understand a grammatical correction or you are unsure which option to choose, click on **About this Sentence** for a detailed explanation.

2 To run through all your mistakes in one go, click the **Tools** menu and select **Spelling and Grammar**.

Suspect words or phrases are displayed in the 'Not in Dictionary' panel, with alternatives listed below. You can 'Change' or 'Ignore' these words or phrases in just this instance, or every time they appear in your document.

3 You can change your spelling and grammar options to suit. From the **Tools** menu select **Options**, then the **Spelling and Grammar** tab. To select an option, put a tick in the box.

Click the down arrow beside 'Writing style' and choose a style from the drop-down menu. This dictates how your grammar is checked.

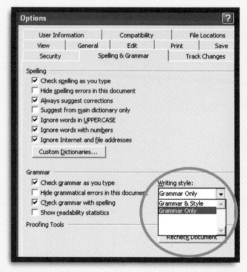

Turn off the spell checker

If you find the Spelling and Grammar checkers' red and green underlining distracting, you can turn it off.

Go to the **Tools** menu and select **Options**. In the 'Options' dialogue box, click the **Spelling & Grammar** tab. Click the check boxes to remove the ticks beside 'Check spelling as you type' and 'Check grammar as you type'.

Watch out

Check words typed in capital letters manually, as Word is not usually set up to examine these. Also look out for any words that you have inserted using WordArt. The program sees these as images rather than words, and they are therefore bypassed by your spell checker.

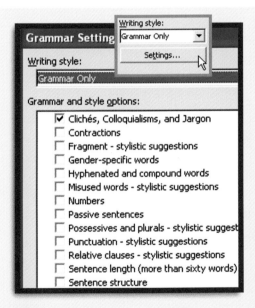

5 If, for example, you often use technical words, you can create your own custom dictionary to prevent the spell checker marking correctly spelt words it doesn't recognise. Under the 'Spelling & Grammar' tab, click **Custom Dictionaries**. Click **New** and type a name in the 'File name' panel. Choose where to save your dictionary and then click **Save**.

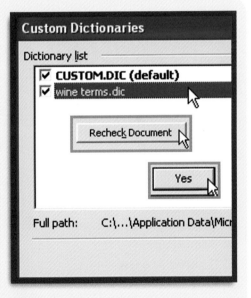

4 You can further adjust your chosen 'Writing style' by clicking the **Settings** button. Here you can opt to check for clichés, 'wordiness', commas, clarity of meaning and so on. You can even choose whether to have one or two spaces after a full stop. Click **OK** when you're happy with your options.

6 Now check the box beside your new custom dictionary in the 'Dictionary list' and click **OK**. If you want to spell and grammar check your document again, adding words to your new dictionary, click the **Recheck Document** button, and then click **Yes** in the following dialogue box.

Thesaurus and Word Count

Sometimes it can be hard to find the right word, or you can find yourself using the same one repeatedly. If you are stuck for inspiration, you can try a thesaurus for an eloquent alternative. A faster solution, however, is to consult Word's own Thesaurus. There is also a word counting facility, which can help you stick to a brief when writing essays or reports.

SEE ALSO...
- *Spelling and grammar* p 58
- *Find and replace* p 64

BEFORE YOU START
Go to the **Tools** menu, click **Language** and **Set Language**. In the dialogue box, select the language you wish to use. Remember that UK and US English are different.

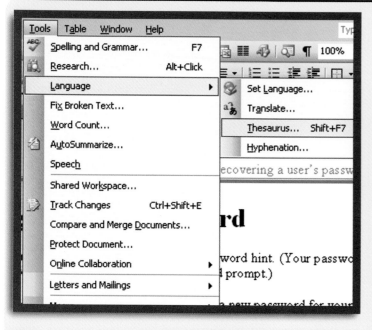

1 Open an existing document that you wish to edit, or type your text. Now highlight the word you wish to look up in the Thesaurus. Go to the **Tools** menu and select **Language**, then **Thesaurus** this opens the 'Research' Task Pane. Alternatively you can use the keyboard shortcut to the Thesaurus, **Shift + F7**.

2 Displayed under 'Thesaurus: English (U.K.)' are possible definitions of your word, indicating whether they are verbs (v.) or nouns (n.) and so on. Hover the mouse over a synonym and click on the arrow to the right to display your options.

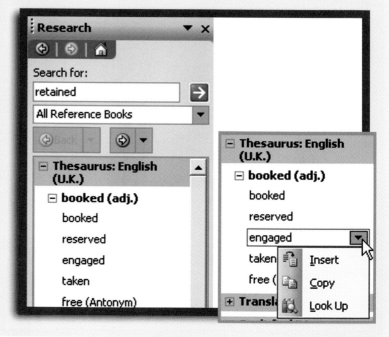

Count your words

For a detailed breakdown of your document, go to the **Tools** menu and select **Word Count**. The Word Count box will display the number of pages, words, characters, paragraphs and lines in your document. Click **Close** to exit.

If you want a breakdown of just part of your document, highlight that section, then go to the **Tools** menu again and select **Word Count**.

Word Count		
Statistics:		
Pages		2
Words		374
Characters (no spaces)		1,858
Characters (with spaces)		2,223
Paragraphs		12
Lines		37

☐ Include footnotes and endnotes

Show Toolbar   Close

That's amazing!

You can use the Thesaurus to look up a word that is not already in your document. Place your cursor on a blank section of the page and open the Thesaurus. Type your word in the 'Search for:' panel, and click the ➜ button to the right. The synonyms and antonyms for that word will appear in the panel below.

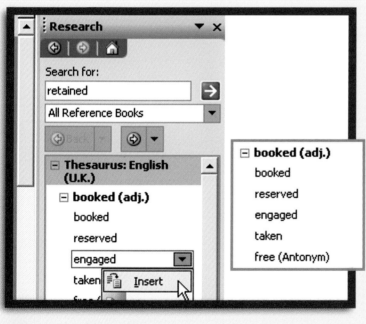

4 You can also look up alternatives for any of the synonyms in the list of results.

Select a word and click on the down arrow to the right and click **Look Up**. Your selected word will now appear in the 'Search for' panel, with a new list of synonyms in the panel below.

To return to your previous search and its alternatives, click the **Back** arrow.

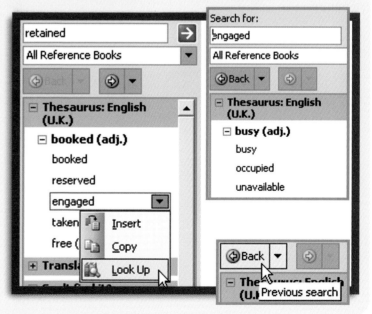

3 If you want to replace your original word with the selection, click **Insert** or **Copy**.

If you want to use a different word, scroll down the list of synonyms and click on your preferred choice.

Note that a word listed with '(Antonym)' after it has the opposite meaning to your word.

AutoCorrect your text

Word's AutoCorrect feature detects and corrects common spelling mistakes, grammatical errors and incorrect use of capital letters. Furthermore, if you know that you often make specific typographical errors, such as typing "seperate" instead of "separate", you can add them to a list – AutoCorrect will then rectify the mistakes for you automatically as you type.

SEE ALSO...
- *AutoFormat* p 46
- *Spelling and grammar* p 58

MAXIMUM EFFICIENCY

To make the most of the AutoCorrect feature, you should set it up to suit your own work requirements.

Go to the **Tools** menu and choose **AutoCorrect Options**. Select the **AutoCorrect** tab. The first four boxes relate to ways in which AutoCorrect

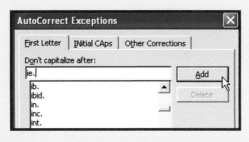

can help with capitalisation. The most useful options are 'Capitalize first letter of sentences' and 'Capitalize names of days'. Click on a box to select it.

It is a good idea to set up exceptions to the

rule. To do this, click on the **Exceptions** button and select the **First Letter** tab. There is a list of abbreviations in the 'Don't capitalize after' panel. To add to it, click in the top panel and type in any word commonly followed by a full stop – for example, the abbreviation 'ie'. Click **Add**. To get rid of an item, select it and click **Delete**.

The 'INitial CAps' tab allows you to make exceptions to the autocorrection of two capital letters at the beginning of a word. The third tab, 'Other Corrections', is for any words that AutoCorrect might detect as misspelt, but which

you do not wish to be changed. Click **OK** to return to the AutoCorrect dialogue box.

Correcting common misspellings

In the AutoCorrect dialogue box under the 'Autocorrect' tab, click in the box next to 'Replace text as you type' if it isn't already selected, then look at the list of possible substitutions in the panel below.

The first few entries are keyboard formulas that you can enter to get certain symbols – for instance, if you type **(c)**, Word will replace it with ©. Scroll down the list to see a number of common misspellings and typing errors that will be corrected

Watch out

When you enter words you commonly mistype in the 'Replace' panel, remember to make sure that they are not actual words – that is, those you might find in the dictionary. If they are, you may find some of your text has been corrected in error after you run AutoCorrect.

Bright idea
If you often use other styles of typed letters, such as superscript for fractions and dates, typing them into the AutoCorrect box saves having to select your text and change style manually.

for you automatically if you use this option. You can even edit words in this list.

Select a word, click in the 'Replace' or 'With' panel, and type in your amendment. Then click on the **Replace** button. You can also **Delete** any spellings that are irrelevant to your work.

To add your own words, type your misspelling in the empty 'Replace' panel, and type the

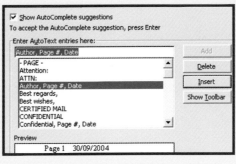

correction in the empty 'With' panel. Click **Add** to add it to the list.

If you select 'Automatically use suggestions from the spelling checker', AutoCorrect will use corrections offered by the dictionary. Be aware that you might not always agree with the dictionary's substitutions, so it is a good idea to check any changes made as you type.

AUTOTEXT

Use this feature to save time when typing dates, letter openers and closers, and other phrases you regularly use.

Select the **AutoText** tab and click the box next to 'Show AutoComplete suggestions'.

When appropriate, a 'ScreenTip' pops up as you type, offering to fill in relevant text – such as today's date. Scroll down the 'Enter AutoText entries here' menu to view a selection of

frequently used words or phrases. To add your own word or phrase to the list, type into the blank panel under 'Enter AutoText entries here' and then click **Add**.

Add a paragraph to AutoText

It is a good idea to add sentences or paragraphs you use often, such as your address, to AutoText. In your document, type some text you often use. Highlight it, go to the **Insert** menu and click **AutoText**, then **New**, to open the 'Create AutoText' dialogue box. The first couple of words are selected as the AutoText name, but you can

change this. Click **OK**.

If you selected the 'Show AutoComplete tip for AutoText and dates' box, simply type the first few letters of the phrase or name of your AutoText entry. A ScreenTip will appear showing your text. To accept the entry, press **Return**. If you did not select the 'Show AutoComplete for AutoText and dates' tip box, go to the **Insert** menu, select **AutoText**, then the name of your entry. It will appear on the page.

Put AutoText on your toolbar

For easy access, you can add the 'AutoText' button to your toolbar. Go to the **Insert** menu and select **Autotext**, then **AutoText** again. Click the **Show Toolbar** button.

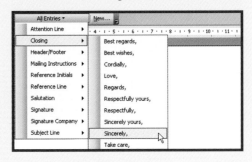

Click the **AutoText** toolbar button to open the 'AutoCorrect' dialogue box. Click on **All Entries** to view and select entries. To add a new entry, highlight your phrase and click **New** to open the 'Create AutoText' dialogue box. Click **OK** to save.

AutoSummarize

AutoSummarize scans your document and picks out the key points. It's useful for providing a summary of reports or any other kind of structured article.

Click the **Tools** menu and select **AutoSummarize**. You're given four summary options: highlighting key points; creating a new document containing the summary; inserting the summary at the top of the existing document; or hiding everything except the summary. Click the option you wish to view. Click **OK**.

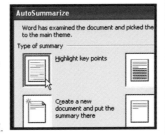

Bright idea
If you accept the first few words of your text as a name when creating an AutoText entry, when you start to type those words, the ScreenTip will automatically pop up.

Find and replace

When editing your work, you may realise that you have consistently misspelt a name or used the wrong sort of formatting. Or you may import a document from another program and find it is full of unwanted formatting and characters. Word's 'Find and Replace' feature allows you to correct these errors with just a few keystrokes.

Close up
To run just a simple search, you can click the Find *tab instead. Or, select the* Go To *tab to find a specific location in your document, such as a page, line or comment.*

BEFORE YOU START
Go to the **Edit** menu and choose **Find** to open the 'Find and Replace' dialogue box. Select the **Replace** tab. This offers the most flexible search and text editing options.

1 Type your search word in the 'Find what' panel. Type a replacement word in the 'Replace with' panel. Click **Replace**. The search word will be highlighted in your document. Click **Find Next** to leave text unaltered, **Replace** to change it to the replacement word, or **Replace All** to replace all instances of the search word.

2 Click **More** for further options – for instance, 'Match case' makes the search sensitive to capitals; 'Sounds like' will search for words that sound the same but are spelt differently. The 'Special' button enables you to search and replace items like paragraph and tab marks, fields and page breaks.

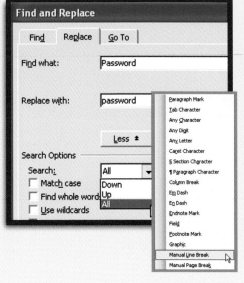

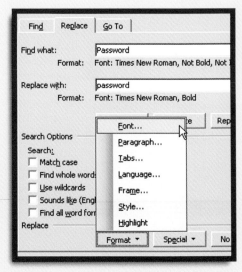

3 To search for formatted text, type your text in the 'Find what' panel, click **Format** and select your settings. To replace formatting, type your text in the 'Replace with' box and go to **Format** again. To search for and replace formatting alone, click in each of the panels before selecting a 'Format' option, but do not enter text.

Customising Word

Change your preferences

Word comes with predefined settings suitable for general word processing use. However, you can change these settings if you feel that others would be more useful. For example, if the ruler at the top of the screen measures in inches, but you prefer to work in centimetres, it is a simple matter of changing the measurement setting to your choice.

SEE ALSO...
● *Spelling and grammar* p 58
● *AutoCorrect* p 62
● *Edit a toolbar* p 68

YOUR CHOICE

In the Tools menu, click Options. Here, you can customise common tasks, such as editing, saving and printing your work, so that they are carried out automatically in the way you prefer.

Viewing options

You will see a dialogue box with three rows of tabs which give you access to preference options.

You will want to change some preferences more than others. Click on the **View** tab. This dialogue box is divided into four sections, and allows you to alter how a page looks on screen. Clicking on any box adds a tick, which means that particular option has been selected.

The uppermost section, 'Show', allows you to select whether to see screen items such as the Status bar, vertical and horizontal scroll bars, screen tips and other page-related options, such as highlights and bookmarks.

'Formatting marks' lets you determine which invisibles are shown, for example, paragraph or tab marks. This is useful for document layout and it is a good idea to tick the **All** box.

'Print and Web Layout options' and 'Outline and Normal options' determine which formatting objects are visible when working on a document.

General options

Use the 'General' tab to change measurement units from inches to centimetres or millimetres, or the typesetting measurements from points to picas. You can also choose how many entries you want to show in the 'Recently used file list' – at the bottom of the 'File' menu – which provides you with a quick way of opening a document that you have recently worked on.

Customising toolbars

To change your toolbar options, click on the **Tools** menu and select **Customize**, then the **Toolbars** tab. Ticking a box next to a toolbar's name means that this toolbar will appear automatically when you launch Word. You can click on as many toolbars as you need.

Clicking on the **Options** tab allows you to change the appearance of your toolbars' drop-down menus and the size of your toolbar icons.

Edit preferences

Editing functions, such as selecting, cutting and pasting text and styling paragraphs, can all be modified in this section.

For instance, if you select the 'Drag-and-drop text editing' box, you can highlight text in your document, then just click and drag it to place it somewhere else. If you select 'Overtype mode', then you can type straight over existing text,

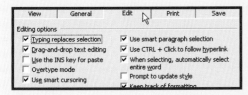

without highlighting it. Click 'Use smart cut and paste' for spaces to be added or removed as necessary when you move text around.

Printing and saving

If you find that you have to change the setup in 'Print' dialogue boxes, or to save and make backups when working in Word, it may be more efficient to set your printing and saving preferences here. For instance, you can save on ink if you print out all

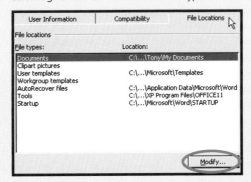

your documents as 'Draft', selecting a higher quality only for letters and other important items.

Spelling and Grammar preferences

You can specify whether you want Word to indicate spelling or grammar errors as you type. You can also select a UK or US dictionary to check your spelling.

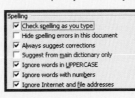

File locations

When you save something, Word anticipates where you will wish to save it. For instance, you might save your documents into the 'My Documents' folder. You can change these locations by clicking the **Modify** button and selecting folders for the different file types.

Compatibility preferences

If someone sends you a Word file that is in an older version, click on the drop-down menu under 'Recommended options for' and select the

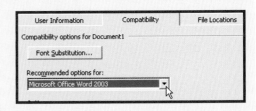

appropriate version. In the 'Options' panel, Word selects the viewing choices it recommends for this document. This affects the way the file appears on screen, but doesn't permanently alter the file.

User information preferences

Each time a document is saved, user information is added to the file properties, such as the name of the person who created that document and their e-mail address. Use this dialogue box to update that information.

Tracking text changes

'Track Changes' allows you to monitor alterations to a document in different ways – for example, by underlining inserted text in red or striking through deleted text in green. This is particularly useful if more than one person is working on the same document, and making lots of changes.

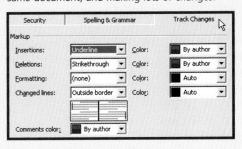

Watch out

Beware of the save option 'Always create backup copy'. You could end up with lots of copies of the same file piling up on your hard disk, so make sure you delete them regularly. For long-term file backups, always save to another disk, such as a floppy or Zip.

Close up

Using the 'Spelling & Grammar' tab, under 'Grammar' options, you can override a previous spelling check, and re-check a document – for instance, if you do not want your grammar checked as you work.

Edit a toolbar

Toolbars are the rows of buttons at the edges of your window that you click on to perform commands. If you position your mouse pointer over a button, you can see a description of its function. There are 16 basic toolbars, each devoted to a particular aspect of word processing. You can add buttons to an existing toolbar or create your own toolbar from scratch.

SEE ALSO...
- Explore the program p 16
- WordArt & Autoshape p 80

BEFORE YOU START
Three toolbars and a ruler normally sit at the top of the Word window.

From the top, you will see the Menu bar, then the Standard toolbar, and finally the Formatting toolbar.

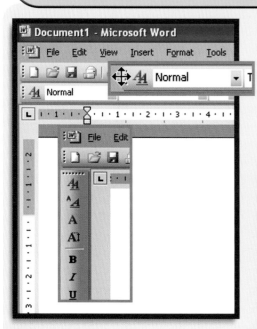

1 To move any toolbar, click its 'Move' handle – the blue dotted bar on the far left – and drag it to a new location. You can move a toolbar to any position on your screen, or swap its position with one of the other toolbars.

2 Click on the small arrow on the far right-hand side of any toolbar and then on **Add or Remove Buttons**. You will see a menu of all the buttons available for that toolbar. On the left of each icon is a small box which is ticked if the button is already selected and present on the toolbar.

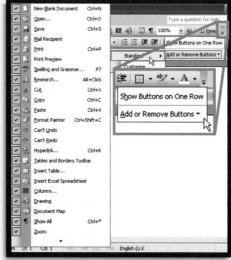

3 To add or remove a button from the toolbar, click the relevant item once. A tick will appear if you're adding a button, and disappear if you are removing it.
   Click **Reset Toolbar** to return the toolbar to its default settings. When you've finished making changes, click on the window to return to your document.

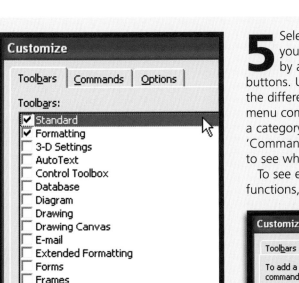

4 To display more toolbars on screen, go to the **Tools** menu and select **Customize**. Under the **Toolbars** tab is a list of all Word's toolbars. The ticked items are already available.

Click any of the items on the list to select or deselect them. Click **Reset** to go back to Word's default settings.

5 Select the **Commands** tab. Here you can further customise toolbars by adding more specialised buttons. Under 'Categories' is a list of all the different types of commands – 'File' menu commands, fonts and so on. Select a category, then scroll through the 'Commands' list in the pane on the right to see what is available.

To see every single one of Word's functions, select **All Commands**.

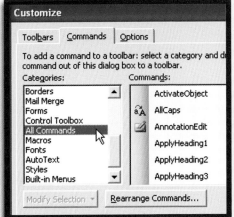

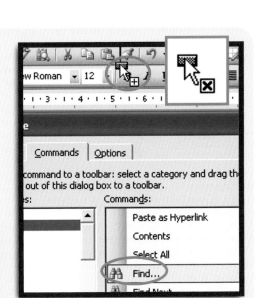

6 To add a command to a toolbar, select the item from the list and drag it onto a toolbar in Word's main window. If you put it in the wrong place, just drag it to a different position.

With the 'Customize' dialogue box open, you can also delete buttons. Just click and then drag and drop the button off the toolbar.

Toolbars for special tasks

Extra toolbars appear automatically when you perform certain functions, such as adding headers and footers, or creating a box with the 'Text Box' tool on the 'Drawing' toolbar. Some of these are displayed only while you are working on the particular feature and disappear when you click on a different part of the document. Others can be added to your current selection of toolbars to make repetitive tasks simpler.

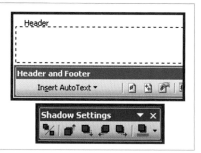

Bright idea
If you find you now have too many toolbars, go back to the Toolbars tab and select only Standard, Formatting *and* Menu bar. **Click on** Reset *and then on* OK *to return the original settings.*

7 To create your very own toolbar, which you can assign to a template or an individual document, select the **Toolbars** tab and click the **New** button. Type an appropriate name in the 'Toolbar name' box and click **OK**.

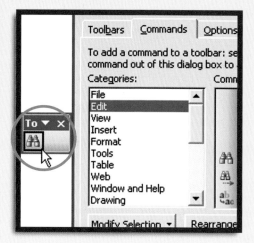

8 Your toolbar is added to the list, and appears to the side of the 'Customize' dialogue box as a small blue square. Select the **Commands** tab. Choose a Category, then click and drag the buttons you want, one at a time, from the list on the right onto your toolbar. You can edit and change an individual icon by selecting it, clicking on **Modify Selection** and then on the appropriate command.

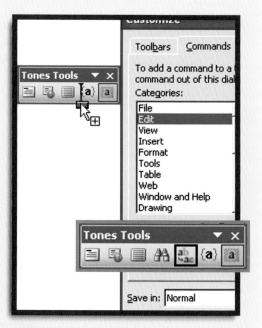

9 When you have finished, click **Close**. Your toolbar is now displayed on the screen. Click and drag it to the position you want it to occupy. You can select it or deselect it in the same way as the other toolbars.

TOOLBARS GALORE

Make yourself familiar with the toolbars available to find out which will be of use to you. There are some you will probably never use, while others will save you a tremendous amount of time when you want to do certain tasks. Do not be afraid to edit toolbars to make them work for you.

DRAWING

Add all kinds of designs and embellishments to personalise your documents.

WORDART

Commands to incorporate a host of special typestyles.

WEB

Facilitates surfing on the Web and stores favourite addresses.

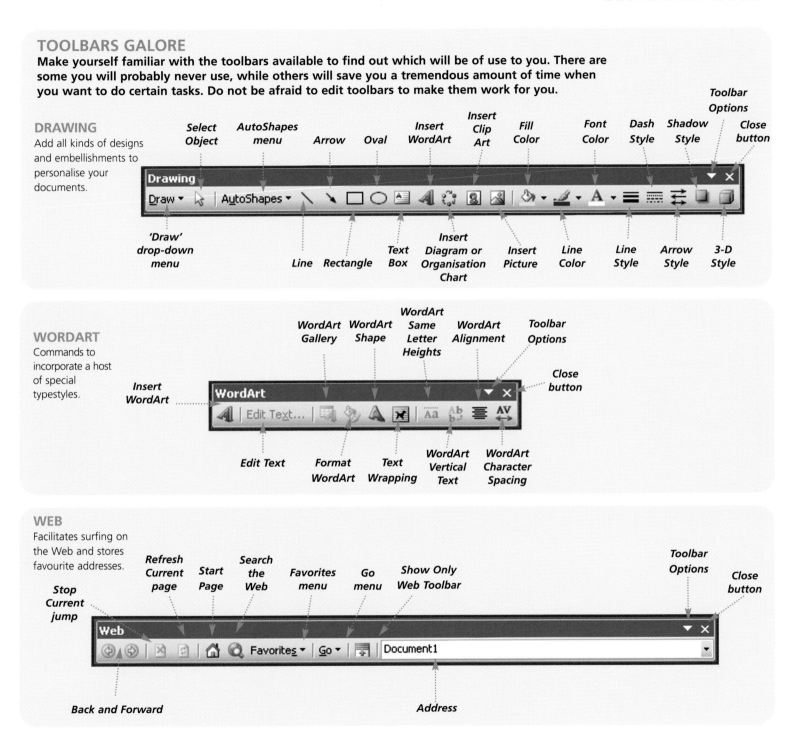

Viewing options

There are several different ways of viewing the document on your screen. If you are designing a Web page, making a brochure or writing a letter, you will probably want to see what it will look like when it is printed or published. Having an overview of the document will also make it easier to restructure it. Find out how Word's options can make your work easier on the eyes.

SEE ALSO...
- *Print your work* p 24
- *Create a Web site* p 98

CHOOSING YOUR VIEW

'Normal View' is the default setting for seeing documents on screen but there are several alternatives.

To access the options for viewing your document, click on the **View** menu and choose a format.

Normal

In 'Normal' view, the text fills the space available in the window and the various toolbars are all accessible. Page and section breaks are indicated by a dotted line. However, in 'Normal' View some graphics and layout features do not appear or are not obvious.

Web Layout

This view enables you to see what the features of the Web page you are creating will look like when it is published on the Internet.

To see your layout in the Web browser, click on the **File** menu and select **Web Page Preview**.

Print Layout

This allows you to work on and view your document as it will look when printed. The whole page is displayed, including margins, headers and footers, columns, and pictures you have added.

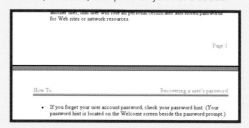

Reading Layout

If you are opening a document simply to read it, this view is the best. To maximise the readability of the document, it hides all toolbars except for the Reading Layout and Reviewing toolbars.

Outline

This structural overview only shows headings. A new toolbar opens up and you can write, select, edit and style all your headings at once, or individually. To restructure the entire document, click on the symbol to the left of a heading, and drag it to a new position.

Full Screen

This is a 'click on', 'click off' function available in the various views. All menus and toolbars are removed, so your document fills the entire screen.

Zoom

A magnifying lens can be found in all the views. It allows you to enlarge or reduce text. Use 'enlarge' if you find yourself peering at the screen or want to work in detail on an image. Use 'reduce' to view whole pages.

Expert advice
You can quickly enlarge or reduce your view of the screen. Just click on the down arrow on the far right of your 'Formatting' toolbar and select a higher or lower percentage of the document size.

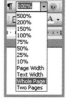

Bright idea
Instead of using the 'View' menu, click the shortcut icons on the bottom left of your screen. Hold the pointer over the button to see what each one does.

Using Graphics

Add a picture

Inserting graphics or pictures into a document can instantly add impact and clarity to your subject. You can either use your own pictures, or choose from the vast gallery of ClipArt provided by Word. Desktop publishing is also made easy by allowing you to integrate illustrations and charts with your text, to produce professional-looking results.

SEE ALSO...
- *Create a newsletter* p 76
- *WordArt & AutoShape* p 80
- *Add a background* p 82

BEFORE YOU START

Open a document. You may already have a picture that you want to insert but don't worry if you haven't – you can easily find graphics stored on your computer, on a CD or on the Internet.

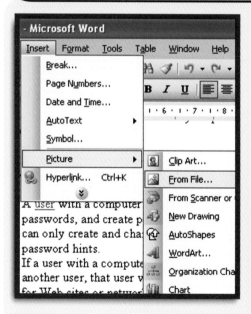

1 To add a graphic to your document, first position the cursor where you would like to insert the image. Next, go to the **Insert** menu and select **Picture**. If you wish to use an image on your PC, a CD-ROM or a floppy disk, select **From File**.

2 The 'Insert Picture' dialogue box appears on screen. It automatically shows the 'My Pictures' folder, where you'll see some sample images. Click the 'Look in' panel's drop-down menu to browse for your image file.
Note that graphics are previewed on the right of the 'Insert Picture' dialogue box. To view a file, click it once. To select it, click **Insert**.

3 Alternatively, to insert a picture from Word's Clip Gallery, go to the **Insert** menu and choose **Picture** then **Clip Art**. The 'Clip Art' Task Pane appears. Type a keyword into the 'Search for' box. Then select where you want to search in the 'Search in' panel.

Text-Wrapping

You can wrap the text around the graphic in different ways by right-clicking on the graphic, selecting **Format Picture**, then choosing the **Layout tab**. Here you will see a variety of wrapping styles. Select one and click **OK**.

Watch out

Although it is fine to use ClipArt in documents such as newsletters and flyers, it is not legal to use it for promotional or marketing material, nor can you publish a document containing it.

5 Only the most common ClipArt files are installed and available instantly on your computer. Sometimes, when you click on your chosen picture you may be asked to insert your Word CD in order to download that clip.

For even more clip options click on 'Clip art on Office Online' if your PC is Internet ready.

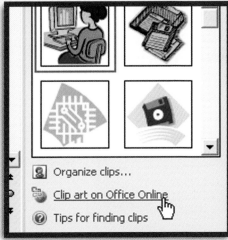

4 Now click on the **Go** button next to your keyword. Your results will be displayed as thumbnails in the panel below. Hover your mouse over a thumbnail for information on that clip. Select your choice of picture and click insert.

6 To resize the image, click on it then using a handle (above), click and drag. The picture toolbar (that automatically appears) is used to adjust brightness, contrast and colours.

If required, right click on the image to Edit the picture. Experiment to achieve different effects (inset).

Create a family newsletter

One of the best ways to keep family members in touch, no matter how far apart they are, is by compiling a regular newsletter. The first task is to ask your relatives whether they would like to contribute any news, such as a new job or a recently passed exam, favourite recipes, or even poems they have written. The rest takes just a few steps in Word.

SEE ALSO...
- *Using columns* p 38
- *Spelling and grammar* p 58
- *Create a Web site* p 98

BEFORE YOU START
Open a new A4 document, name it and save it. Go to the **File** menu and click on **Page Setup**. Select the **Margins** tab, then set the sizes for the 'Top', 'Bottom', 'Left' and 'Right' margins. Click **OK**.

1 Type in your heading, then press the **Return** key. Type in all of your articles, giving each its own title. Press the **Return** key between each article to leave a line space. Once all of your text is typed, you can run a spell check. In the **Tools** menu, click on **Spelling and Grammar** and check for any suspect words.

2 Add a ClipArt image (see page 74). Click on it and go to the **Format** menu and select **Picture**. Click the **Layout** tab, then the **Advanced** button. Select the **Text Wrapping** tab and click on **Tight**. Click the **Picture Position** tab and tick 'Move object with text', so the image is locked to the paragraph of text around it. Click **OK** twice.

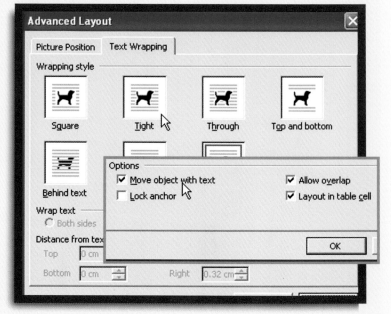

Applying settings
To apply your column settings to the area of the document below the heading, click on the arrow to the right of the 'Apply to' panel, scroll through and select **This point forward**.

4 Text is usually easier to read if you set it out in columns. Place the cursor at the start of your first article, go to the **Format** menu and click on **Columns**.

Select **Two** in the 'Presets' section. Set the column width and spacing. To run a vertical line between the columns, ensure the 'Line between' box is ticked, then click **OK**.

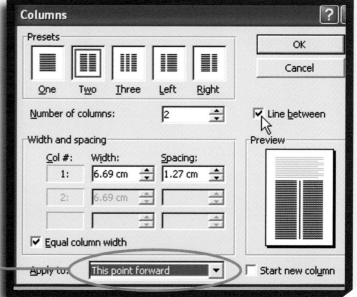

3 Highlight your heading and go to the **Format** menu, then click on **Font**. Choose a font, style, size and colour. As this is an informal document, choose a fun font. You can see how it looks in the 'Preview' panel.

For a distinctive look, check the 'Shadow' box and select a dotted rule in the 'Underline style' box. Click **OK**.

Adjusting line spacing

To adjust line spacing, highlight the article (not the heading), click on **Format** then **Paragraph**. Under 'Spacing', click on the down arrow in the 'Line spacing' panel, and select an option. If you know which point size you want, click **Exactly** and select the size in the 'At' panel.

To increase the space between paragraphs by a further 1 point at a time, click on the up arrow next to the 'After' panel. Click **OK**.

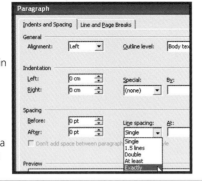

Close up
To use photographs in your newsletter, scan them in, or get them scanned at a bureau, and save them on your PC. Go to the Insert menu, select Picture then click From File. Find your photograph and click Insert.

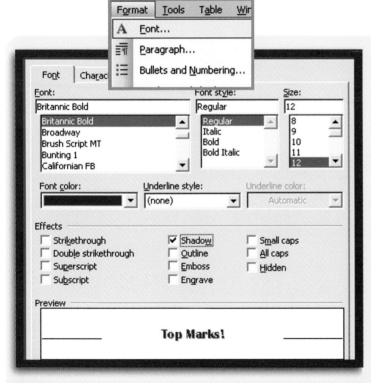

5 Highlight the heading of your first article, go to the **Format** menu and select **Font**. Now choose a font, style, size and effect.

If you are printing in colour, click on the arrow to the right of the 'Font color' panel, scroll through and pick a colour. Click **OK**.

6 Now highlight and style the first paragraph of your first article in the same way. Choose a bold font style to make it stand out. Continue to highlight and

style the rest of the text and headings using similar fonts, styles and sizes.

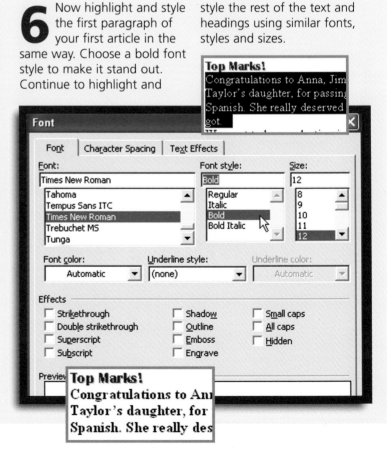

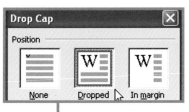

Drop Caps
In the 'Drop Cap' dialogue box, click on the **Dropped** icon in the 'Position' section. Select the number of lines you want it to drop by in the 'Lines to drop' panel to adjust its size, and click **OK**.

8 If you want to produce a regular newsletter, save your document as a template. Go to the **File** menu and select **Save As**. Scroll though file options in the 'Save as type' panel and select **Document Template**. Word will save your newsletter in its 'Templates' folder ready to use for your next edition. Finally, click on **Save**.

7 To add a large capital letter at the start of a paragraph, click your cursor in the paragraph, go to the **Format** menu and select **Drop Cap**. Apply the settings in the dialogue box (see 'Drop Caps', above), and click **OK**.
   To preview how your document looks, go to the **File** menu and select **Print Preview**.

WordArt and AutoShape

You can make text behave like a graphic image if you use WordArt. Just pick one of the predefined styles and type in the word you wish to use. You can then reshape and resize it, and wrap normal text around it. AutoShapes are graphics such as stars, arrows and smiley faces. You can add them to your document, and position and size them to suit your page.

SEE ALSO...
- *Edit a toolbar* p 68
- *Add a picture* p 74

 BEFORE YOU START
With your document open, go to the **View** *menu, click on* **Toolbars** *and select* **Drawing**. *When you are editing graphics, it is always useful to have the Drawing toolbar on screen.*

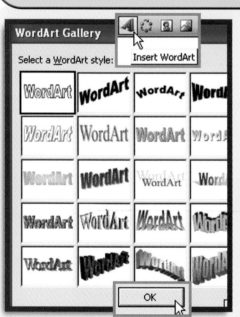

1 To insert WordArt, click on the page roughly where you want your WordArt text to appear. Now click the **Insert WordArt** icon on the Drawing toolbar. Choose a style from the 'WordArt Gallery', and click **OK**.

2 The 'Edit WordArt Text' dialogue box appears, with the words 'Your Text Here' highlighted. Type your own words over them.
   At the top of the box are 'Font' and 'Size' panels, and 'Bold' and 'Italic' buttons. Use them to style your text. When you are satisfied, click **OK** to view the WordArt in your document.

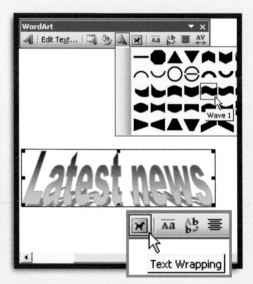

3 With the WordArt selected, you can move and resize it like a graphic (see page 75). If the WordArt toolbar is not visible, go to the **View** menu and choose **Toolbars** then **WordArt**. Using the WordArt toolbar, you can edit your words, change the style and shape of your graphic and choose how text on the page wraps around it.

Editing graphics

The Drawing toolbar allows you to edit or format your graphics. Click the **Draw** button to view some of the options. Click on **Order** to place one graphic behind another or behind text. Select **Rotate or Flip** to change the orientation of your graphic. Click **Text Wrapping** to choose how graphic and text interact on the page, and use **Change Autoshape** to replace your AutoShape with another.

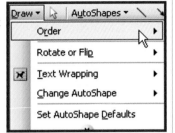

That's amazing!
You can even add text to an AutoShape. Right-click on the shape and choose **Add Text** from the pop-up menu. All you have to do is type in the text and it will wrap automatically inside the Autoshape.

1 To insert an AutoShape into your document, go to the **Insert** menu, choose **Picture**, and select **AutoShapes**. The AutoShapes toolbar appears on screen with buttons representing the shape categories. Click the buttons to view the choices.

2 Try clicking on the **Basic Shapes** button and choosing **Smiley Face**. To place it, click where you want it to appear in the document.

Hold the pointer over a round 'handle' until it changes to a double-headed arrow. Then click and drag to size your AutoShape. The width to height ratio will be preserved if you hold down the **Shift** key while dragging the handle.

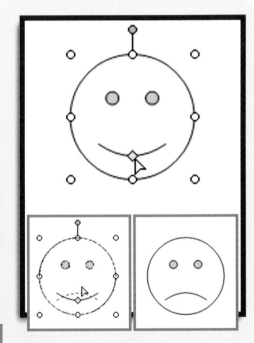

3 To change the Smiley Face to a Sad Face, select it, then click on the yellow diamond in the centre of the mouth and drag it up, so that the corners of the mouth turn down.

Add a background

Giving your document a coloured or textured background is a great way to liven it up. You can write over the top, insert picture and text boxes and use the document as the basis for Web page design. Although you cannot print Word's 'Backgrounds', the 'Watermark' function enables you to print a faded version, ideal for creating stylish personalised stationery.

SEE ALSO...
- *Design a letterhead* p 42
- *Headers and footers* p 52
- *Add a picture* p 74
- *Create a Web site* p 98

WHICH BACKGROUND?

Use the 'Background' feature to create coloured and textured pages for files that you don't need to print out.

With your document open, go to the **Format** menu and select **Background**. To add a solid colour to your document, just select one from the

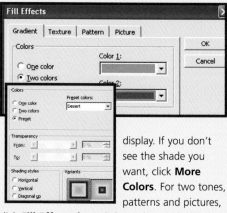

display. If you don't see the shade you want, click **More Colors**. For two tones, patterns and pictures, click **Fill Effects** for a dialogue box with more options. Select the **Gradient** tab. Click the radio buttons to choose one or two colours and the 'Color 1' and 'Color 2' panels to select which ones. Click the **Preset** radio button for a panel of themes such as 'Desert' or 'Sunset'.

'Shading styles' changes the way the two colours are mixed. View 'Variants' on the right

and double-click to select a background.

For other options, click the **Texture** tab and choose a preset background or click the **Pattern** tab and select a colour from the 'Foreground' and 'Background' panels, then double-click on a pattern box to select it.

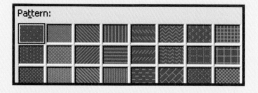

If you want to insert an image file as your page background, click the **Picture** tab, then **Select Picture** to open the dialogue box. Images stored in 'My Pictures' are listed. Select a picture, click **Insert**, then click **OK**.

PRINTABLE BACKGROUNDS

Word's 'Watermark' feature places a faded version of your chosen graphic on the page, which can be printed.

Go to the **Tools** menu, select **Customize** and ensure the 'Drawing' and 'Picture' toolbars are selected, then click **Close**. The two toolbars will appear on screen. Now go to the **View** menu and select **Print Layout**.

Insert Picture

Here, you can view both text and Watermark. Go to the Picture toolbar and click the **Insert Picture** icon. Use the 'Look in' panel to locate your image, then click **Insert**.

Click on the picture in your document. Hold your pointer over the handle until it becomes a double-headed arrow. Click and drag to resize.

Select the picture, and on the Picture toolbar, click the **Color** icon, then select **Washout**. The cursor is at the bottom of the image. Select the **Text Wrapping** button and click **Behind Text** to bring the cursor to the top. Click on the image and reselect **Behind Text** so that you can write on top of the watermark.

Click on the page and press the **Spacebar** or **Tab** key before using the **Return** key to position your text.

Headers and footers

Insert a watermark to run as a Header or Footer, appearing on every page. Go to the **View** menu and select **Header and Footer**. Using the Picture toolbar, insert, size and watermark your image. Use text wrapping to add text over or beside your picture inside the Header or Footer box.

Special Functions

Mail Merge

When you need to send the same letter to lots of people, using the mail merge facility is a fantastic time saver. You can create one letter and merge it with a data file of all the relevant names and addresses. You can use this feature for all kinds of mass mailings, whether you're writing to family and friends, club members or business contacts.

SEE ALSO...
- *Address labels* p 86
- *Use macros* p 90

BEFORE YOU START
You may wish to use data such as names and addresses from Microsoft Access, but you can also create a new data source while setting up the mail merge (see page 86).

2 Under 'Select starting document' choose an option. Use the current document; Start from a template; or Start from existing document. Choose 'Start from a template', for example, then click on 'Select template'. From the 'Select Template' dialog box, choose a template, then click **OK**. Edit your document using the prompts. Then to go to **Step 3** click Next: Select recipients.

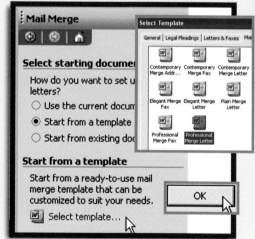

1 Open a new document, go to the **Tools** menu and select **Letters and Mailings** then **Mail Merge**. From the Task Pane under 'Select document type' choose **Letters**. Then click Next: Starting document to go to **Step 2** of the wizard.

3 Under 'Select recipients' choose an option, 'Use an exisiting list', for example. Click **Browse**, then from 'Select Data Source' dialogue box, select your list file, and click **Open**. The 'Mail Merge Recipients' dialogue box displays your list. Edit it if necessary and click **OK**. Go to **Step 4**. Next: Write your letter.

That's amazing!
Use Mail Merge to print addresses directly onto envelopes. In Step 1, after selecting **Envelopes**, click **Next** and then **Envelope options** to choose envelope size and orientation. Click **OK**. Click **Next** to move to Step 2. Follow the remaining steps through selecting the various options as you go. Finally click Next: Complete the merge to finish.

Close up
You may need to alter some field names. Take time to think about those relevant to your own data, removing any you do not want, typing over and adding others and leave an extra one, which you can edit later.

Bright idea
Always check your work before you print, Step 5 Preview your envelopes*, option lets you check your results, before you waste costly stationery. Plus you can always* Edit individual envelopes *if you so wish.*

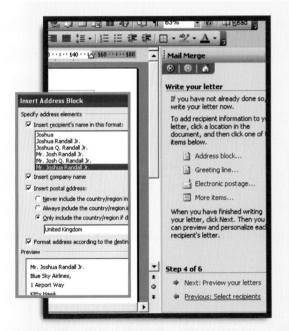

5 Here under 'Preview your letters' you can see how your letters will look before you print them. Also under 'Make changes' you can Edit your recipients list or 'Exclude this recipient', that is the one you are viewing.
Finally go to **Step 6**. Next: Complete the merge.

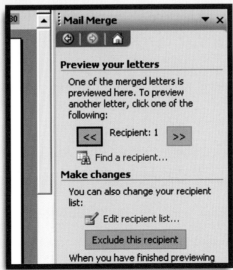

4 Add additional information to your letter by clicking on the options under 'Write your letter'.
When you are satisfied with your letter customisation, go to **Step 5**. Next: Preview your letters.

6 If required, you can personalise your letters, by clicking 'Edit individual letters'. This will open a new document for your merged letters.
Alternatively, under 'Merge' click 'Print'. This brings up the 'Merge to Printer' dialogue box, make your choices and click **OK**. Then click **OK** again to print.

Make address labels

Addressing numerous envelopes is a repetitive and time-consuming task. However, Word's label printing feature can save you a lot of effort and makes your envelopes look professional. If you already have address lists stored on your PC, you can use the merge feature to print the details as labels, or create sheets of address labels for individual contacts.

SEE ALSO...
- *Wizards & templates* *p 50*
- *Mail merge* *p 84*

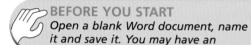

BEFORE YOU START
Open a blank Word document, name it and save it. You may have an address list already, but don't worry if you haven't – we'll show you how to do this with the 'Mail Merge Wizard'.

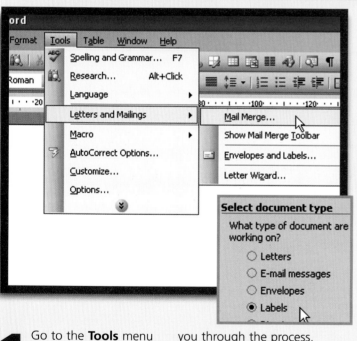

1 Go to the **Tools** menu and select **Letters and Mailings** then **Mail Merge**. The 'Mail Merge' Task Pane wizard will appear on right of your screen to guide you through the process. Under 'Select document type' click on 'Labels'.
At the bottom of the pane click Next: Starting document to go to **Step 2** of the wizard.

2 Step 2, under 'Select starting document' choose an option. 'Change document layout' or 'Start from existing document' to modify an existing mail merge document. We'll use 'Change document layout' for this example. Now under 'Change document layout' click on 'Label options' to select you label size.

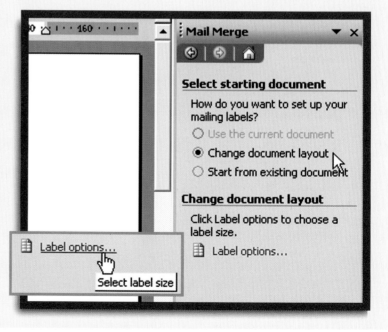

New label

If your label type is not listed, you will need to enter the details. In the 'Label Options' dialogue box, click on the **New Label** button and, following the diagram, add the label sizes and give it a name. Click **OK**.

Key word
A field marks a place in your document. When you perform a merge, the fields instruct your program where to put the information you're merging into your document, such as names and addresses.

Close up
Sheets of address labels come in various sizes. Each page size and configuration of labels has its own reference number. For A4 printers, one of the most popular is the L7163, with 14 labels on an A4 sheet.

4 Your original blank document now displays a grid of blank labels set out in columns and rows according to your label selection.
Click Next: Select recipients to go to **Step 3** of the wizard.

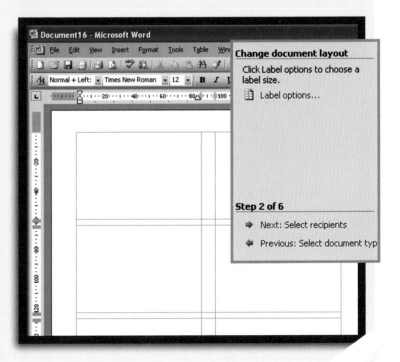

3 The 'Label Options' dialogue box displays various options. Select a manufacturer from the 'Label products' panel and choose the correct label from the 'Product number' list. Click **OK**.
Alternatively, click **New Label** (see above). When finished click **OK**.

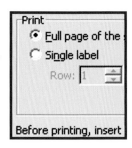

Expert advice
To print a one-off label, or a whole
sheet of the same address, go to
the **Tools** menu and select **Letters
and Mailings** then **Envelopes
and Labels**. Click on the **Labels**
tab and type your information into the
'Address Area'. Click the **Options** button, select
your label type and click **OK**. Now opt to print a full
page of the same label, or single label. Click **Print**.

Print
- ● **F**ull page of the
- ○ **Si**ngle label
  - Row: 1

Before printing, insert

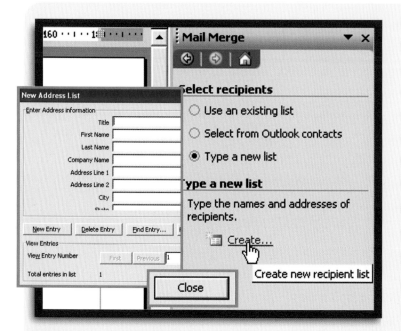

6 The 'Save Address List'
dialogue box appears.
Key in a name for your
file and click **Save**.
Automatically the 'Mail
Merge Recipients' dialogue

box appears. Check the details
of your list are correct, make
any adjustments and click **OK**.
At the bottom of the pane
click Next: Arrange your labels
to go to **Step 4**.

5 Under 'Select recipients'
you can choose to use
an existing list of names
and addresses or select 'Type a
new list', if you don't already
have one. To generate a new

list, click on 'Create'. The
'New Address List' dialogue
box appears. Fill in the fields
and then click 'New Entry' to
add another, and so on. When
finished click **Close**.

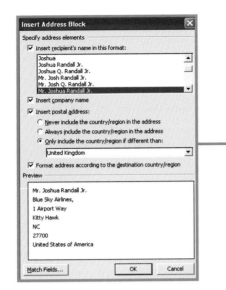

Watch out

Before you print the whole list of address labels, it's a good idea to do a test run on plain paper. You only need to print out one page of addresses to check that it is laid out as you want. To do this, click on **Pages** under the 'Page range' section in the 'Print' dialogue box, and type '1' in the panel beside it. Click **OK**. Only your first page of labels will print.

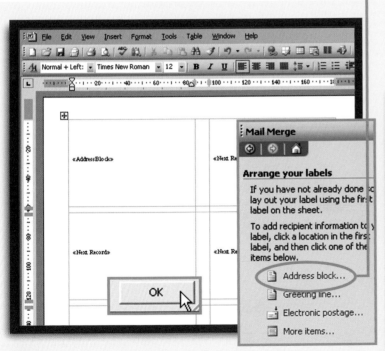

8 Check your labels, and make any adjustments. Click Next: Complete the merge. Click 'Print'. The 'Merge to Printer' dialogue box appears. Check your 'Print records' settings and click **OK**. Click **OK** again to print.

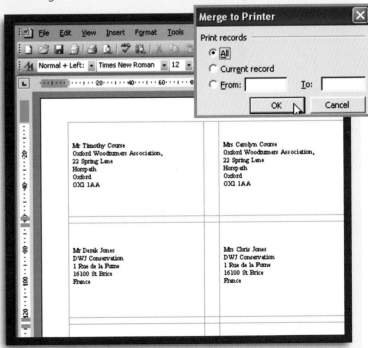

7 You can lay out your label by adding items like 'Address block' to the first label. In the 'Insert Address Block' dialogue box choose your address elements and check your results in the 'Preview' pane. Click **OK**. Now click Next: Preview your labels to go to **Step 5**.

Use Macros

If you have a particular piece of text or an item, such as a table, that you often use in documents, it makes sense to save it as a macro, instead of creating it from scratch each time. Then, whenever you wish to add that item to a page, you just simply run your macro. A macro can be assigned to a menu, a toolbar, or a combination of keystrokes.

SEE ALSO...
- *Design a letterhead* p 42
- *Edit a toolbar* p 68

BEFORE YOU START
Decide exactly what you want to save as a macro and how you want it to look, whether it is your name and address or a table with a specific number of rows and columns.

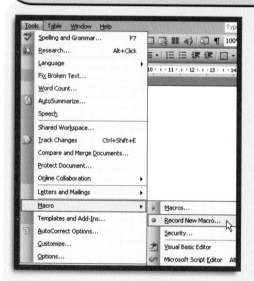

1 To create a macro you need to record all of the instructions you would normally use when you are creating your chosen item. These can then be played back instantly, at any time, to recreate it. Go to the **Tools** menu and choose **Macro** then **Record New Macro**. The 'Record Macro' dialogue box will appear on screen.

2 Name the macro, choosing something that reminds you of its function. Under 'Store macro in' you can select 'All Documents' to save your macro in Word's blank document template, or just add it to the document you're working on.

To assign your macro to a toolbar or create a keyboard shortcut for it, click the **Toolbars** or **Keyboard** icons.

3 If you clicked the **Toolbars** icon, you'll see your macro in the 'Commands' panel. Click and drag it onto the toolbar or menu in the main window to which you wish to assign it.

To create a keyboard command for your macro as well, click the **Keyboard** button. Otherwise, click **Close**.

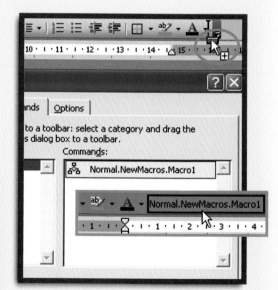

Editing Macros

If you want to change some of the text contained in a macro, go to the **Tools** menu and select **Macro**, then **Macros**. Choose the relevant macro and click the **Edit** button. Any text shown in quotation marks can be highlighted and typed over, as normal.

If you wish to change commands in your macro, it is easiest to delete your macro and recreate it from scratch.

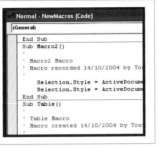

Watch out

Macros can be used to spread computer viruses, so if you open a file created by someone else, and a dialogue box appears, asking whether you want to enable macros, the file could have a virus. The safest option is to not enable the macro and to check the file with your anti-virus software before you open it.

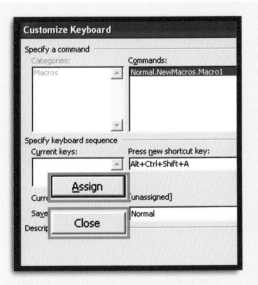

4 In the 'Customize Keyboard' dialogue box, type a keyboard command that will activate your macro into the 'Press new shortcut key' panel – for instance, **Alt + Ctrl + Shift + A**. You can see below whether this command is assigned to another function or not. If it is 'unassigned', click the **Assign** button, then **Close**.

5 The Macro toolbar appears on screen. It is very small and has two buttons – click the left button to stop recording and the right button to pause. Click again on the right button to resume recording.

Create the item that you wish to include in your macro. When it looks exactly how you want it, click the **Stop Recording** button.

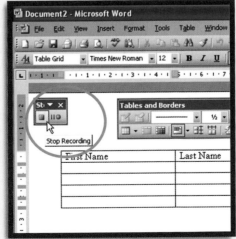

6 The next time you wish to add that item to a document, click the toolbar button or menu to which you assigned your macro, or press your keyboard command.

Alternatively, go to the **Tools** menu and click on **Macro**, then **Macros**. In the dialogue box is a list of available macros. Click on your macro and select **Run**.

Sort a list

Word enables you to sort information contained in lists or tables. For example, you may want to make a list of the members of your local club and sort it alphabetically by name. You can also sort by date or number in ascending or descending order, but you need to ensure that you have defined and identified the criteria and format for your sort.

SEE ALSO...

● *Using tables* p 48

BEFORE YOU START
Be aware that if you type a space at the beginning of a word, it will appear first in the list, as a space comes before 'A' in the alphabet, as do punctuation, symbols or numbers.

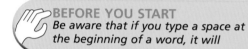

1 To sort a list of names alphabetically, type in the first names followed by the surnames in any order. Press the **Return** key after each entry. When the list is complete, highlight it, go to the **Table** menu, and select **Sort**. In the 'Sort Text' dialogue box, the default setting is to sort your list from A to Z, by the first word of each entry. If this is what you want, click **OK**.

2 To sort your list by surname, click the **Options** button. Below 'Separate fields at', select the **Other** radio button and type a space in the panel on the right. Click **OK**. Back in the 'Sort Text' dialogue box, click on the drop-down menu below 'Sort by' and select **Word 2**. Ensure **Text** is chosen in the 'Type' panel. Click **OK** to initiate the sort.

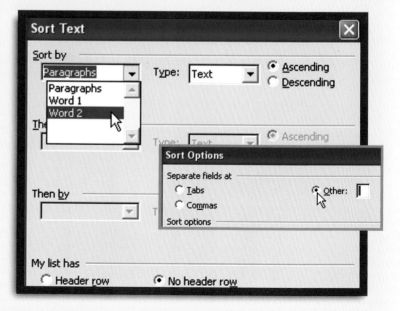

Bright idea
For easier sorting, convert a list to a table. Highlight the list, go to the Table menu, click Convert*, then* Text to Table*. Use the dialogue box to format the table and specify how entries should be separated into cells.*

Watch out
If you want to sort a mixed list by numbers, make sure you specify Number in the 'Type' panel, so that the sort function ignores everything in the list except numbers. If Word sorts your numbers as text, number 1 will be followed by 10, 11, 12 and so on. The number 2 will come after 19!

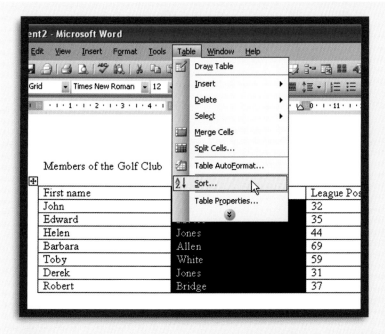

4 You can choose to sort in ascending or descending order. If you have selected more than one column, you can set the order of your sort – for instance, sorting the data first by column two, then by column three. If you have selected your column headers, click the 'Header row' radio button in the 'My list has' section, so that your headers don't get sorted as well. Click **OK**.

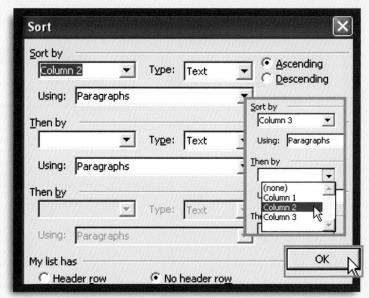

3 If you have a table of information, you can easily reorganise your columns using the Sort feature. Highlight the cells to be sorted, or highlight a whole column by positioning the insertion point at the top of the column and clicking when it changes to an arrow. Go to the **Table** menu and select **Sort**.

Doing a calculation

One of Word's useful features is that it offers some of the functions of a spreadsheet package, such as Excel. It enables you to perform calculations and you can also use formulas in many ways. You can calculate your personal expenditure, develop a table for basic bookkeeping or work out a business plan.

SEE ALSO...
- *Using tables* p 48
- *Sort a list* p 92
- *Import & export files* p 96

BEFORE YOU START
You will need an empty row in which to put the formula's result. Position the cursor where you want to insert a row, go to the Table menu, select Insert then Rows Above.

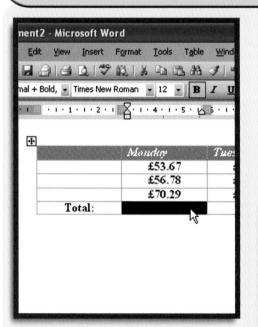

1 To create a formula to add up a column of numbers in a table, click on the empty cell below the column. Go to the **Table** menu and select **Formula**. The 'Formula' dialogue box appears on screen.

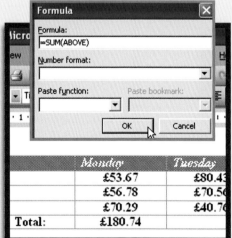

2 The 'Formula' panel says '=SUM(ABOVE)'. This means that it is offering to add up the cells in your column. The equals (=) sign always starts a formula. 'SUM' means addition. '(ABOVE)' means that the formula applies to all the cells above your selected cell.
Click **OK** to activate the formula. The total immediately appears in your table.

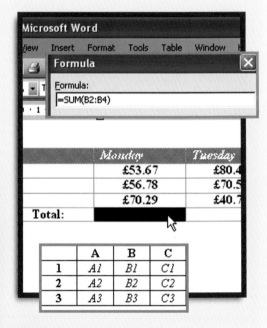

3 Alternatively, you can specify a range of cells on which to carry out a function by enclosing them in brackets in the 'Formula' panel. Cells are described using letters for columns and numbers for rows.

Different calculations

You can do more than simple addition in your tables. Here are some of the options available in the 'Paste function' menu: 'SUM' is for addition, while 'MIN' finds the lowest value and 'MAX' finds the highest value.

To multiply values use 'PRODUCT' and to find the number of items in a list use 'COUNT'.

You can round numbers to a specific decimal place using 'ROUND(x,y)' where 'x' is the value and 'y' is the desired number of decimal places.

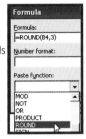

That's amazing!
You can use the 'AutoSum' button on the 'Tables and Borders' toolbar to add up a column or row of figures automatically. Just click on the empty cell and then on the **AutoSum** button.

5 Click the down arrow beside 'Paste function' to reveal a choice of functions. Scroll down and select **Average** – it will appear in the Formula panel. Now type '(ABOVE)' or type the range of cells between brackets.

You can also choose how the numbers are displayed in your table by clicking the drop-down menu below 'Number format' and selecting one of the options.

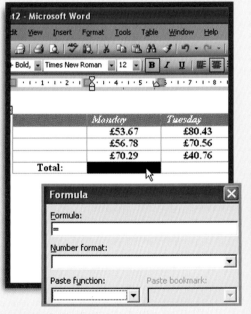

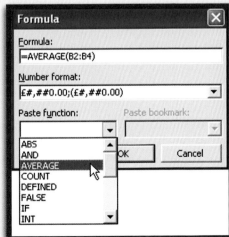

4 To use a function other than 'SUM', highlight the cell in which you want the result to appear. Go to the **Table** menu and click **Formula**. This time delete the formula offered to you, leaving the equals sign in place.

6 If you change the formula or any of the figures on which the formula is based, the result will not change until you update the formula. To do this, right-click on the formula cell and select **Update Field**.

Import and Export files

Importing files into Word from other Microsoft programs, such as Excel and Access, is a good way to present different kinds of information as well as creating an interesting document with lots of visual impact. Likewise, exporting Word files into another program, such as PowerPoint, allows you to display your work in different formats.

SEE ALSO...
- *Save your work* p 22
- *Using tables* p 48
- *Add a picture* p 74

FILE FORMATS AND CONVERTERS

The process of importing and exporting files is not complex. However, certain programs have format restrictions.

Word is primarily a text-based program, whereas Access and Excel are database programs, which means that information is divided into cells, fields and records.

When you import an Access file into Word, you can style it using Word's table formatting options.

However, when you import an Excel table, it is already formatted as a spreadsheet. Once imported, you can only alter its size and where it appears on the page. For the same reasons, you can only export a Word file designed as a table into Access.

Many programs have powerful converters for translating text and images from other file formats. When you try to import a file, your

computer will prompt you if it needs to use a converter. If the converters are not installed on your PC, then the program will ask you to install one. Program converters are stored on your Word or Office CD-ROM. Insert the CD in its drive and follow the step-by-step instructions that appear.

IMPORTING FILES INTO WORD

Recent versions of Word let you build multimedia Web pages. As a result, the program recognises and can incorporate many file types in standard documents.

Excel into Word

To insert an Excel worksheet, open a Word document, go to the **Insert** menu and choose **Object**. Select the **Create from File** tab. In the 'File name' panel you will see '*.*', which means 'all files'. Either type the

specific file name over this, or click **Browse** to view a list of your files. Highlight the file to be

inserted and click **Insert**. Click **OK**. Click on a handle and drag to resize the table.

Access into Word

To bring an Access table or query (specified data from a database) into an open Word document, go to Word's **View** menu, click **Toolbars**, then **Database**. On the toolbar, click the **Insert**

Bright idea
The quickest and easiest way to copy small amounts of information from one program to another is to use the 'Cut' and 'Paste' functions, which you'll find in the 'Edit' menu.

Close up
To import an Excel worksheet quickly into a Word document, click the Insert Microsoft Excel Worksheet button on Word's Standard toolbar.

Database button. In the 'Database' dialogue box click **Get Data**, then click and scroll down the 'Files of type' panel at the bottom of the window. Select **Access Databases** so you can view available files. Highlight your file and click **Open**. In the 'Microsoft Access' dialogue box, check that

the table or query you require is highlighted and then click **OK** to return to the 'Database' dialogue box.

Choose **Query options** if you want to filter the data by applying a query. This defines exactly which data you want to insert. Click the **Table AutoFormat** button and scroll through the 'Formats' panel to choose a style for your table. Once you have chosen a style, click **OK** to return to the 'Database' dialogue box.

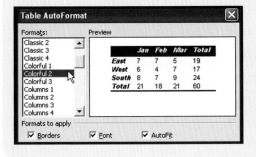

Click the **Insert Data** button. Another dialogue box offers the default choice of 'All' records. Click **OK** to insert the table into your Word document.

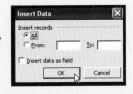

As with a table that you create in Word, you can resize the imported table by clicking and dragging on the handles. You can also click in any cell to edit the data it contains, and use the **Table** menu to insert and delete rows and columns (see page 48).

EXPORTING WORD FILES
Specialised programs, such as PowerPoint and Access, vary in the degree of difficulty involved in exporting a Word document into them.

Word into PowerPoint
It is easy to export files from Word into PowerPoint, which is a program for combining text and multimedia for making presentations.

Click on **Open** in the PowerPoint **File** menu. In the 'Open' dialogue box, select **All Files** from the 'Files of type' panel. Locate and double-click

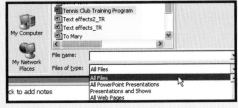

on your Word document. PowerPoint will then automatically convert the document into a format that you can manipulate and make into a professional-looking presentation.

Word into Access
You can import information into Access from Word, but only if you want it to appear in a database format. Therefore, you need to enter the text in the Word document with this in mind. Open a new Word document, type the headings for your records, such as 'Name' and 'Address', and separate each with a comma. Press **Return** before you begin to enter the individual information for each record, also separated by commas. Press **Return** after typing the information for each record. When you have entered all the information, save the document as a 'Text Only' file.

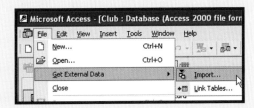

Open Access and go to the **File** menu then **Get External Data**, and **Import**. Locate and double-click on your text file. Make sure the 'Delimited' option is selected in the 'Import Text Wizard' dialogue box, and click **Next**. Click in the 'First Row Contains Field Names' box, and click **Finish**, then **OK**. The information from your Word document will be displayed in a database.

Early versions of Word
If you are sending a file to someone who uses an earlier version of Word, they may have difficulty opening it because of formatting differences. Use the 'Save as' function in the 'File' menu to save it as a file type that is easy to open, such as 'Plain Text' which removes the formatting. To avoid problems when importing files created in an earlier version of Word, open them using the 'File' menu within Word. In the 'Files of type' panel select the version of Word for the file you wish to open. Word will be able to recognise and open it.

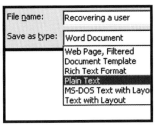

Set up a family Web site

O ne of the most exciting projects on a PC, if you can access the Internet, is to create your own Web site. It is a great opportunity to trace long lost family members or to promote a club or society to an audience of millions. You can design your site using Word in a matter of minutes, and then connect to the Net and publish your pages.

SEE ALSO...
● *Save your work* p 22
● *Wizards & templates* p 50

BEFORE YOU START
You will need Web space from your Internet Service Provider. To get this, contact your ISP. You will be allocated a few Megabytes of space on their server, as well as a Web address.

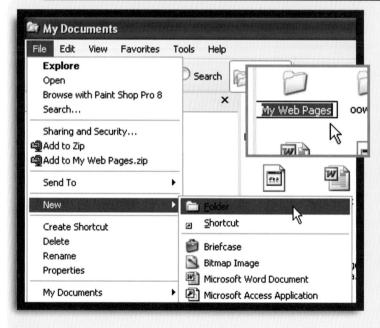

1 It's a good practice to keep all your web pages together. So, from your 'My Documents' folder, go to the **File** menu and select **New**, then **Folder**.

Right click on 'New Folder' icon and select **Rename** to give your folder a suitable title, 'My Web Pages', for example.

2 Then with Word running, go to the **File** menu and select **New**. In the 'New Document' Task Pane under 'Templates' click 'On my computer'. From the 'Templates' dialogue box click on the 'General' tab and select **Web Page** then click **OK**.

Bright idea
Word offers a variety of design elements to use on your own Web pages. You can also obtain backgrounds, buttons and rules from various Web sites, and disks that come free with PC magazines.

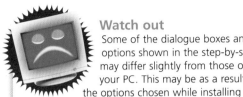

Watch out
Some of the dialogue boxes and options shown in the step-by-step may differ slightly from those on your PC. This may be as a result of the options chosen while installing Windows or Office, or caused by software updates received over the Net. However, this will not affect your ability to complete the project.

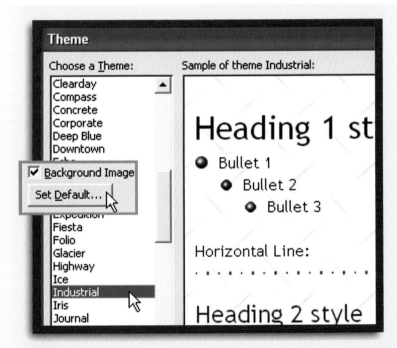

3 Go to the **Format** menu and select **Themes**, to choose a visual theme for your site. Make your selection and click **OK**.

To use your selected theme throughout your site, click **Set Default**. Then click **Yes** in the 'Set Default Themes' dialogue box. Then click **OK**.

4 Now type in your main heading text. Click on the **Center Align** button. Highlight your heading, go to the **Format** menu and select **Font**. Choose a font, style, size, colour and effect. View your styling changes in the 'Preview' pane. This text will remain constant at the top of you web site. Click **OK**.

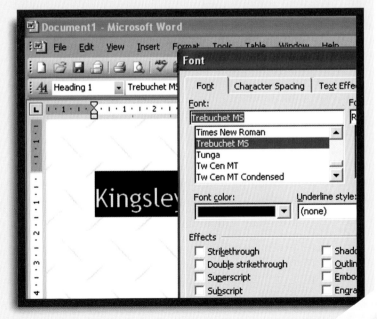

Key word
The term homepage refers to the page that is designed as the first page you'll see when you visit a Web site. However, a homepage can also stand alone, without other pages being linked to it.

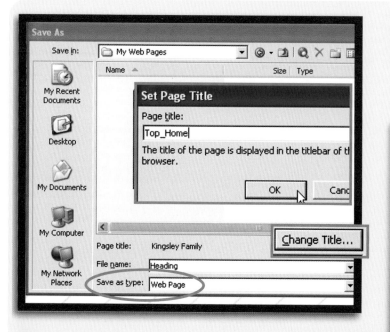

6 Click on the **New Web Page** icon to start a new page using your chosen 'Theme'. Now key your 'Homepage' text (the page that is displayed when your Web site is first browsed). Save the file as in Step 5. Continue to create and save your web pages – Contents, History, Celebration – for example, in the same manner.

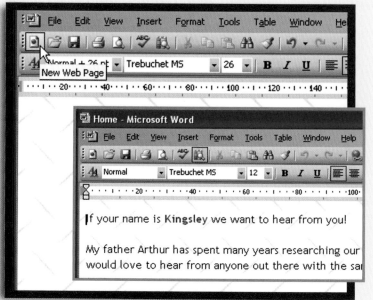

5 Save this page in your 'My Web Pages' folder in the normal manner, making sure you select 'Web Page' in the 'Save as type' drop-down panel.

Click on 'Change Title' to give your page a meaningful name when displayed in the title bar of a web browser. Click **OK**. Then click **Save** to finish.

Key word
A Web frame is used to make information easier to access, or to display the contents of a Web site that has multiple pages. Using Web frames organises information and gives your site a more professional feel.

Close up
When you divide a single Web page into sections that can each display a Web page, each section is called a frame. The container that holds the group of frames is called a frames page.

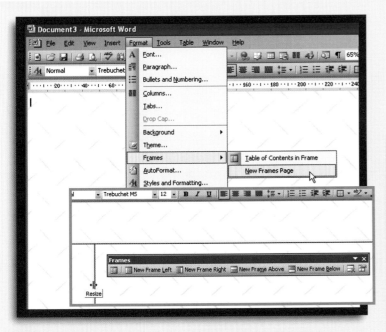

8 Click inside the top frame and then from the 'Frames' toolbar click **Frame Properties**. The 'Frame Properties' dialogue box appears. Click the **Frame** tab and then the **Browse** button, and navigate to, and select your 'Header' page to be displayed in that frame.

Click the **Borders** tab to style your borders width and colour, and to select other frame options. Click **OK**.

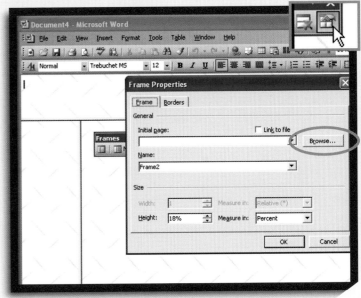

7 Create a new blank Web page. From the **Format** menu select **Frames** then **New Frames Page**. The 'Frames toolbar' appears. Click **New Frame Above**, to create a 'Header' frame. Click below your header frame and click **New Frame Left**, to create your 'Contents' frame. Drag the border to resize a frame.

Key word
A hyperlink is a feature built in to many sites that allows you to move from one location to another, either on the same Web site or on a completely different Web site, with a single click of the mouse.

Expert advice
To remove a hyperlink from your Web page, highlight the words that activate the link, go to the **Insert** menu and select **Hyperlink**. In the 'Edit Hyperlink' dialogue box, click on the **Remove link** button.

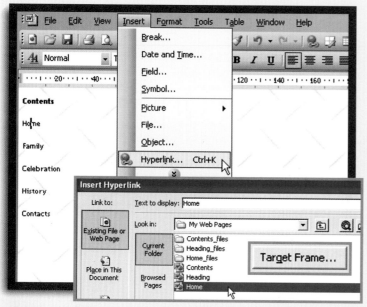

10 The 'Set Target Frame' dialogue box appears, which lets you select a frame to display your linked page. The Target Frame default is (Main). Click in the 'Current frames page' preview to select your target frame. Check the 'Set as default for all hyperlinks' box. Repeat for the other 'Contents' items. Click **OK**. Save your 'Frames Page' as a 'Web page' (see Step 5).

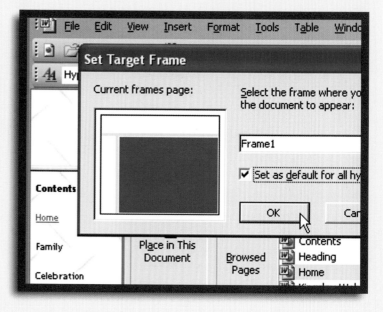

9 Now click in your left frame, and from the 'Frames' toolbar, click on the **Frame Properties** button (see previous Step) to insert your 'Contents' page.
To add a hyperlink, click on 'Home', for example. Go to the **Insert** menu and select **Hyperlink**. From the 'Insert Hyperlink' dialogue box navigate to and select your 'Home' file, then click on **Target Frame**.

Key word
Copying your Web pages to a server is called uploading because you are moving documents from an individual computer to a large network. When you download, you are doing the opposite.

Watch out
You will need to rename your 'Frames Page' to either index.html or default.html before you upload it to your allocated folder on your hosts server. Check which naming convention they use before you upload.

12 Finally, to upload your web pages, click in the address bar of your web browser, and type **ftp.yourdomain.com** where 'yourdomain' is <u>your</u> host's name. The 'Log On As' dialogue box appears to type in your 'User name' and 'Password'. Click **Log On**. Then drag and drop your files into your allocated folder.

11 Now open your Web browser and type the name of your frames page into the address bar and press **Return**. Your site will be displayed – just as Web users around the world will see it. Test your links from the 'Contents' frame to make sure they access the correct page. The site is now ready to upload to your host's server.

A

Active window The window in which you are working. To activate a window, click on it and it will jump in front of any other open windows on screen.

Alignment The position of text and objects on a page in relation to the margins. Text can be aligned to the left or right margin, centred down the middle of the page or justified so that lines of text fit the width of the page, column or box.

Alt key The key to the left of the spacebar on the keyboard that activates a command when pressed in combination with other keys. *See Shift key.*

Arrow keys The four keys at the bottom of the keyboard that move the insertion point up, down, left and right, or allow you to scroll through a window's contents.

AutoFormat This feature is used to apply formatting according to settings that you have created and saved.

Autoshapes A selection of predesigned graphic shapes that you can insert in a document and customise to your needs.

B

Background A colour, texture or image positioned on the page as a layer on top of which all other text and objects sit.

Backspace key This is located in the top right-hand corner of the main block of letter keys on the keyboard, often showing a left-facing arrow. This key deletes text to the left of the insertion point. *See Delete key.*

Bitmap An on-screen image made up of tiny dots or 'pixels'.

Browse (in a window) To search through the contents of your computer, viewing the names of the files in each folder.

Bullet point A small graphic, often a black dot, used to indicate individual statements within a list.

Button An on-screen image on which you can click to perform a function, for example the 'OK' or 'Yes' buttons to confirm an action.

C

Caps Lock Pressing this key will cause all letters that you type to appear as capitals, or in 'upper case'. Press the key again to return to standard characters.

Cell A small, rectangular unit in a spreadsheet, database or table, into which text or figures are entered. Click on a cell to make it active.

Chart A graphic representation of data such as a graph, that can be inserted into a Word document.

Click To press and release the left mouse button once. Menu and dialogue box options and toolbar buttons are selected in this way.

Clip Another word for a ClipArt image. *See ClipArt.*

ClipArt Graphic images that come with the Word program which can be inserted into documents and then resized and manipulated.

Clipboard A virtual location where items cut or copied from a document are stored. The Word Clipboard can store several items of data at a time, regardless of size. Use the Paste command on the Clipboard Toolbar to insert a Clipboard item in a document.

Close A command on the File menu to shut down the active window or document, but not the program. It serves the same function as clicking the 'Close' button in the top right-hand corner of a window.

D

Copy To make a duplicate of a file, image, or section of a document.

Cursor A marker, usually a flashing vertical line, indicating where text or inserted objects will appear. Also called the 'insertion point'.

Cursor keys *See Arrow keys.*

Cut To remove selected text and/or images to the Clipboard, where they are stored for later use.

Database A system for storing data so it can be easily accessed, organised, and sorted. Each entry is called a 'record' and each category in a record is called a 'field'.

Data source A file that contains information stored in database form, such as names and addresses, which can be used in a Mail Merge. *See Mail Merge.*

Default The manufacturer's settings for a program when no others have been specified by the user. For example, Word automatically uses the US dictionary. However, you can change default settings using Options in the Tools menu.

Delete To completely remove a selected file, folder or image, or a piece of text from your document.

Delete key This is located in the group of six keys to the right of the main block of letter keys on the keyboard. This key deletes text to the right of the insertion point. *See Backspace key.*

Desktop The background screen on your PC. It is the starting point for all work. Icons represent various office items, such as files, folders, and a waste basket known as the 'Recycle Bin'. The background is called 'wallpaper', while the Start button gives you access to the programs, your work and the computer's settings.

E

Destination document The file to which an item currently on the Clipboard is to be added. *See Source document.*

Dialogue box A window that appears on screen when you are using a program. It usually asks for preferences or further instructions to be input by the user in order to complete a procedure.

Digital image A picture that is stored in binary format, so it can be viewed and changed on a PC.

Document A single piece of work created in a program, also known as a 'file'.

Dots per inch (dpi) The number of dots per square inch that either make up an image on screen or that a printer has the capability to print. The more dots, the greater the detail and quality of the image.

Double-click To press and release the left mouse button twice in quick succession. This is most often used to open documents and folders, and to activate programs.

Drag A mouse action used to highlight text, reshape objects, or to move an object or file. Click, and keeping the left button held down, move the mouse as required.

Drawing toolbar A supplementary toolbar containing options for adding artistic elements to your Word documents.

Drop-down menu A list of options that appears when you click on one of the headings on the Menu bar.

E

Edit To make a change to an element in a document or to alter the preferences for a program.

End Pressing this key takes you to the end of the line of text on which the cursor is positioned.

Error message A small window on

screen warning that a fault has occurred and, where possible, suggesting an action to remedy it.

Export To save a Word file in a form that allows it to be incorporated in another Microsoft Office application, such as Powerpoint.

External hardware Additional computer equipment attached by cable to a PC, such as a printer.

F

Field A category for information in a database, such as 'Name' or 'Address'.

File Any item stored on a computer, whether it is a program, a document, or an image.

File extension A three or four-letter code assigned to the end of the file name when it is saved. It states the type of file it is so the computer knows in which program to open it. Common extensions are listed here:

File format The way in which files

Text	.asc .doc .html
	.msg .txt .wpd
Image	.bmp .eps .gif .jpeg
	.pict .png .tif

created by different programs are saved. *See File extensions.*

Fill To apply a chosen colour to a designated area. You can also apply a mix of colours using 'Fill Effects'.

Folder An electronic storage location for keeping related files and relevant documents together.

Font A specific style and set of characters for a typeface such as Times New Roman.

Footer A box at the base of every page of a document that contains information relevant to the whole

document, such as page numbers and copyright details. *See Header.*

Format To alter a document's appearance by applying style, typography and layout options.

Form letter A correspondence, created using Mail Merge, which is used to send the same letter to many different addresses.

Formula A set of conditions that carry out a mathematical calculation.

Frame Used to contain a single web page within a frames page.

Full Screen This is the view that increases the size of the active window to fill the screen.

Function keys The 12 keys at the top of the keyboard, ranging from F1 to F12, which perform special tasks.

G

.gif file Graphics Interchange Format. A common file format for storing digital images.

Graphic Any type of digital image on a computer, including pictures, photographs and illustrations.

H

Handle The small squares that appear at the corners and sides of an object when you select it. They allow you to adjust the dimensions of the object by dragging them to a different position.

Header Information which appears at the top of each page of a document.

Help key Usually the F1 key on the keyboard, this accesses advice and information on performing a task.

Highlight To select text, images or cells by dragging the cursor over the item. *See Drag.*

Home Pressing this key takes you to the start of the line of text on which

the cursor is positioned.

Hyperlink A piece of underlined text or an object that you click on to take you to a specific Web page using your Web browser (provided you have access to the Internet).

Hyphen A short 'dash' used to join two words, such as that in 'right-hand'. Word also lets you use a non-breaking hyphen. This prevents a hyphenated word from being split when it appears at the end of a line by taking the whole word over to the next line.

I

Icon A graphical representation of a file or a function, designed to be easily recognisable. For example, the printer icon on the Standard toolbar accesses the print function.

Import To bring text, images or files from another program into a Word document.

Indent To position a line or lines of text further from the page margin than the following or preceding lines. Often used to mark the beginning of a new paragraph.

Inkjet printer A type of printer that works by squirting tiny drops of black or coloured ink onto the surface of the paper. Most home printers use inkjets.

Insert To add an element to a document, such as an image or text. This is best done using the Insert menu.

Insertion point *See Cursor.*

Internet Short for 'International Network'. Millions of computers worldwide linked by telephone and cable lines. Users access the Internet via a phone connection to their ISP.

ISP Internet Service Provider. A company that provides a connection for your computer to access the Internet via a telephone line.

Italic A style of writing whereby the letters are typed with a slight slant to the right. It is most often used to emphasise specific words or phrases, or for the names of books and films.

J

.jpeg Joint Photographics Experts Group. A file format that compresses the data required to make up an image so that it uses less space.

Justify To force lines of text to fit either the space between the left and right margins, or a specified column width.

K

Keyboard shortcut A combination of keys pressed simultaneously to issue a specific command.

L

Laser printer A type of printer that uses a laser to etch images onto a drum and then transfers them to paper, giving a higher quality printout than an inkjet printer.

Layout This refers to the way that items are arranged on a page.

Letterhead A design or information, such as your name and address, that appears at the top of all your letters.

Log on To access a restricted computer, file or Web site using a security procedure, like a password.

M

Macro A series of commands or actions that can be recorded, then activated by a keystroke and played back when required.

Mail Merge A way of incorporating name and address data from another application, such as the Address Book, into Word, allowing you to repeat a letter with the same content but with personalised addresses.

Margins The white space around the edge of the document, the dimensions of which can be adjusted.

Maximise To increase the size of a window so that it covers the entire Desktop area.

Menu bar A toolbar of headings at the top of a program window which displays categorised options in drop-down menus when you click on them.

Minimize To reduce a window to a button on the Taskbar. This allows you to continue running several programs without cluttering the Desktop with windows you are not using at that time.

Modem A device to allow you to connect to the Internet via a telephone line.

Monitor The unit similar to a television which displays all of your work on-screen.

Mouse pointer A small arrow or cursor on screen that moves in relation to the mouse.

Multimedia Computing which combines different methods of communication such as sound, images, text, and video.

My Documents A Windows Desktop icon representing a folder for storing files created by the user.

N

Net Short for Internet. *See Internet.*

Non-printing characters These are symbols that can be viewed in the document on-screen to show word spacing, paragraphs and line returns. They do not appear on the printed document.

Normal View A simplified view used for typing, editing and formatting text. You do not see the page boundaries in this view. *See Print Layout and Reading Layout.*

O

Object A self-contained item that can be placed in a Word document and retains` its characteristics, such as an image or a spreadsheet.

Office Assistant An animated character who offers suggestions and help as you work in Word. The assistant can be switched on and off, and its settings can be altered to suit the way you work.

Online The status of a computer when it is actively connected to the Internet.

Open To bring a file, folder or program into use.

Orientation An option available when creating a document. Users can choose to set up a page as either Landscape (of greater width than height) or Portrait (of greater height than width), depending on how they want the final document to appear.

P

Page break The position in a document at which one page ends and another begins. Insert a page break manually at any point in a document and Word will reposition the elements on the pages to accommodate it.

Page Setup The settings that allow you to specify the layout of your page, margin sizes, paper size and how you view your document.

Page Up/Page Down These keys take you up or down respectively, to the next page of your document.

Panel A space in a dialogue box in which information can be entered.

Paste To insert text or other data that has been cut or copied to the clipboard.

Pixels Individual dots on a computer screen. The greater the concentration of pixels, the higher the level of detail and improvement in the quality of display.

Plain Text The way of saving a text document if you want to open it in another word processor or e-mail program. However, any formatting or styling you applied will be removed.

Point size A standard scale for measuring typefaces. For example, the text on this page is 8 point, whereas newspaper headlines are often 72 point.

Pop-up menu A list of options that appears when you right-click on the Desktop.

Printer driver Software that enables the operating system to communicate with the printer.

Print Layout The document view that shows the page edges so you can see the position of text and objects as you are working. *See Normal View and Web Layout.*

Print Preview The on-screen display of how a document will look when it is printed. Changes cannot be made to the document when using Print Preview.

Properties The attributes of a file or folder, such as its creation date, format and author's name.

R

Radio button A small circle beside an option which you click to activate. An activated option will have a black dot in the radio button.

Range A group of related cells in a table or spreadsheet.

Reading Layout This is the view to simple read a document. *See Print Layout and Web Layout.*

Recycle Bin A Desktop icon and feature used to store files ready for permanent deletion. To delete files in the Recycle Bin, right-click on the Recycle Bin icon and select 'Empty Recycle Bin' from the menu.

Resize To adjust the dimensions of an object in a Word document. Do this by clicking and dragging the handles that appear on its edges when you select the object.

Resolution The degree of detail on a screen or a printed document, measured in dots per inch (dpi). The higher the dpi, the better the detail.

Return key The large key on the right-hand side of the main block of letter keys on the keyboard. Press to create a new paragraph in your text.

Rich Text Format A way of saving a document so that if it is opened in another word processor or Microsoft program, it will retain the formatting and styling that you applied to it.

Right-click To press and release the right mouse button once. In Word, this causes a pop-up menu of options to appear with different options depending on the item on which you clicked.

S

Save To store or copy a document to a disk, most often a floppy or the hard disk.

Save As This function allows you to allocate a name to a file you are saving. It also lets you save an existing file to a different drive or in an alternative format without affecting the original saved file.

Scroll To move through the contents of a window or menu vertically or horizontally.

Scroll bar The grey panel running either down the right-hand side or along the bottom of a window containing a darker grey block. By clicking on the block and dragging along the panel you can scroll down the page or from side to side.

Search A mini-program that searches for a file, usually by its name or creation date. Also, a command which searches a document for specific information, such as a word or phrase.

Select To click on a file, folder, image, text, or other item, so it can be moved or manipulated.

Server A computer that is the main file storage location connected to a network of other computers. To publish your Web site, you will need to transfer your Web documents from your PC to an Internet server.

Shift key Used to type a capital letter when pressed at the same time as a letter key, or to type the symbols on the number keys. It can give you access to program functions when pressed together with other keys. For example, press 'Shift' + 'Alt' + 'T' to insert the current time in your document.

Software Programs designed to perform specific functions. For example, Microsoft Word is software designed for word-processing.

Source document The file from which an item is cut or copied to the Clipboard for use in another document.
See Destination document.

Spacebar The wide key along the bottom of the keyboard for inserting spaces between words.

Spellcheck Checks your spelling and suggests corrections. It can use alternative dictionaries to which you can also add terms.

Standard toolbar The line of small icons in Word that sits at the top of the window below the Menu bar and contains common features used when creating word processing documents. These include Save, Print, Spelling and Grammar checker, and Cut, Copy and Paste.

Start The button on the left of the Taskbar for viewing the Start menu.

Status bar The grey bar along the bottom of program windows containing information about the current document.

Style The appearance of the various elements of a document.
See Format.

T

Tab Short for 'tabulate'. A feature for positioning text at various distances from the left-hand margin.

Tab key The key to the left of the 'Q' key, used to position text at preset intervals across the page. It is also used to move between cells in spreadsheets, or to move from one database field to the next.

Table A group of cells in rows and columns, in which you can type text or place images. Inserting a table in a Word document helps to arrange the elements neatly on the page.

Taskbar The bar usually positioned along the bottom of the screen that displays the Start button, and buttons for programs and documents currently open.

Task Pane A window next to your document displaying your current task options.

Template A format for saving a document so that its elements can be used to create similar documents.

Text break This feature lets you insert a permanent break between lines of text or paragraphs.

Themes Background styles that you can apply to your document. Themes are most effective when used on Web pages as they do not print out on standard Word pages.

Thesaurus An alphabetical list of words and their possible synonyms or antonyms arranged similar to a standard dictionary.

Tile To reduce the size of a group of open windows, arranging them on the Desktop so that they can all be seen at once.

Toolbar A bar or window containing buttons for issuing commands or accessing functions.

Track changes A feature which lets other people add comments to your document without actually making permanent alterations.

Truetype A fonts file that permits characters to have smooth edges no matter how small or large they appear in a document.

Typeface *See Font.*

U

Undo A function that allows you to reverse the last task or several tasks that you carried out.

URL Uniform Resource Locator. The standard style of Internet address for a Web site. The main part of the URL – 'www.name.com' – identifies a virtual location for a group of linked Web pages, known as a 'domain'. Any additional parts – '/myhome/mypage.htm', for example – indicate the location of a specific Web page document within the domain. *See Server.*

V

View A menu of options which allows you to change the way a document is displayed on screen.

W

Watermark A feature that alters an image so that it prints as a faint grey background effect behind the text in a document, thus giving the effect of a stationery watermark.

Web Layout The view for working on Web page documents. *See Normal View* and *Print Layout*.

Window The self-contained viewing and work area of a file or program. Several windows can be open at once on the Desktop.

Windows Explorer A program for viewing the contents of a computer in a single window.

Wizard A program tool that guides users through customising a predesigned document.

WordArt Text created in a graphic form that can be customised and imported into a document for decorative effect.

Word processing Text-based activites on the computer, such as letter writing. Word processing allows you to create professionally styled documents with an wide range of fonts, sizes and colours.

World Wide Web The part of the Internet composed of millions of linked Web pages that can be viewed using Web browsing software, such as Internet Explorer.

Wrapping The manner in which an object, such as an image, is positioned in relation to text. It can sit behind the text or make the text flow around it in various ways.

Z

Zoom To enlarge an area of a document for ease of viewing.

INDEX

Numbers shown in **bold** type are for main references to the subject listed.

A

Access (program) 12, 84
  importing from 96
active window 84, 104
address
  address labels **86-89**
  books 84-87
  Web 71, 98, 102
aligning
  buttons 19, **37**
  decimals 41
  pages **24-25**
  paragraphs 36-37
  using tabs 40-41
Alt key 14
arrow button 71
arrow keys 14
arrows
  double-headed 17, 18, 100
AutoCorrect 62-63
AutoFormat 46-47, 48
  options 47
AutoShape 71, 81
AutoSum 95
AutoSummarize 63
AutoText 63

B

background 82
Backspace key 14, 21
backup
  disk 67
  work 23
blank document 20
  template 50
bold 19, 29
bookmarks 66

borders 49, 53
bullet points 19, 35, **39**
business 40, 42-45, 50, 94-95
  faxes 45, 50
  invoices 40
  letterheads 42-45, 82
  letters 82, 85
  mailing 84-89
  templates 12, 47, **50-51**
buttons
  add/remove 19, 68-70

C

calculations 94-95
  AutoSum **95**
  formulas 94-95
  tables **48-49**
capitalisation 21, 59, 62
Caps lock key 14, 21
cells 49
click (mouse) 13
ClipArt 74-75
clipboard 57
Close button 17
colours 30
  customising 30
  highlight button 19
  printing 26
  text 30-31
columns 38-39, 48, 77, 100
  break 54
  button 19, 39
  ruler 39
commands 12, 66, **69**
  customise 66-69, **90-91**
  issuing 12
  Menu 18
  shortcut keys **14**
  tab 69
  undo 57
copy see cut
  to Web page 57
Ctrl key 14
cursor 17, 20
  double-headed arrow 100

flashing 17
  handle 68
  keys 14
  pencil shape 49
customise 66-73
  bullets 35, 39
  colours 30
  commands 66-69, **90-91**
  spell checker 58-59, 63
  toolbars 66, **68-71**
cut, copy and paste 56-57, 96
  buttons 19, 57
  Clipboard 57
CV 50-51

D

databases see also tables
  Access 84, 96
  address book 84-87
  cells 49, 93
  field 85, 87
  import 96
  inputting 49, 85, 96
  spreadsheets 48-49
  update fields (formulas) 95
  using 85, 88-89
data source 84, 86
date 44, 63
default settings 66
delete
  breaks 54
  text 21
Delete key 14, 21
  screen freeze 22
desktop publishing 74
dictionary 58-59, 67
  customise 59
documents
  appearance 34
  AutoSummarize 63
  draft 37
  new 19
  opening 13, **20**
  outline view 72
  saving **22-23**

  summary 72
  window **17**
drawing
  lines 71
  tables 49
  toolbar 71, 81
drop cap 79

E

edit
  text 56–64
  toolbars 68-71
  WordArt 80
Edit menu 18, 56
End key 14
entering 20
Enter key 14
envelopes 24, 85, 86-89
Esc key 20
Excel 13, 71, **96-97**
exporting
  to other programs **96-97**
  to the Web 98-103

F

family
  finances 94-95
  newsletter 32, 38, 74, **76-79**
  photographs 74, 78, 100
  Web site **98-102**
faxes 13, 45, 50
field 85, 87
File menu 18
files
  backing up 23
  exporting **96-97**
  folders 67
  formats 23, 44
  importing **96-97**
  locations 67, 23
  recently used 66
  renaming 22, 23
  saving 19, **22-23**
Find and Replace 64

floppy disk 23
folders 67
  new 22
  organising 22, 67, 69
fonts 28-32, 42
  character scaling 32
  colours 19, **30**
  panel 19
  serif 29
  sizing 28, 29, 19
  styles **30-32**, 44, 77-78
  symbols 28
  types of 29
Footers *see* Headers
footnotes 52
Format menu 18
formatting
  AutoFormat **46-47**
  borders 49, 53
  columns **38-39**, 54
  documents **34-35**
  graphics 81
  invisible marks 19, **20**, 41, 47,
    54, 66
  paragraphs **36-37**
  replace 64
  section breaks 54
  tables 48-49
  undo 47
Formatting toolbar 19, **34**,
    37, 44
formulas *see* calculations **94-95**
Frames 101-102
Frames Page 102
Function keys 14

G

grammar 58-59
graphics 74-81, *see also* images

H

handle 68, 100, 104
hardware 11
  speakers 11

Headers and Footers 42-43,
    52-53, 82
  toolbar 53
headings 34-35, 47
  summary 72
Help menu 18
hidden text 31
highlight 13
Home key 14
homepage *see* Web
hyperlink 102
  button 19
  remove 102

I

illustrations *see* images
images 74-75,
    77-77 *see also* Autoshape,
    ClipArt, WordArt
  basic shapes 81
  drawing 80-81
  editing 75, 80-81
  fill effects 82
  free rotate button 71
  graphics 74-81
  My Pictures folder 74, 82
  pictures and photos 74-76, 100
  resizing 75, 81, 100,
  rotate graphic 81
  shadow button 71
  toolbars **71**, 75, 80-81
  text wrap 76, 81, 82
importing files 96-97
indents 36-37
  buttons 19
  hanging 36
  markers 37
  ruler 37, 41
  tab settings 40, 41
insertion point 13, **17**
Insert key 14
Internet *see also* Web
  service provider 98, 102
  uploading/downloading 103
invisibles 20, 41, 47, 54
italic button 19

J

justify *see* alignment

K

Keyboard 11, **14**
  shortcuts 14
keys 13, **14**, 21

L

labels 86-89
  mailing 86
  printing 89
  sticky 24, 87-88
language options 58, 60
layout 24-25
  defaults 50
  margins **24**
  page 25
  tabs 24, 25
  templates 50
  view 72
  Widow/Orphan controls **37**
letters *see* stationery
line
  breaks 36-37, 38, 54
  spacing 37, 43, 78
lines
  arrows 71
  styles 71
  wavy red or green 21
lists 40-41, 46, 47, **48-49**
  convert to table 93
  sort **92-93**

M

macros 90-91
  edit 91
  viruses 91
mailing *see* labels
Mail Merge 84-85, 86-89
Maximise/Restore button 17

measurements 41, 66-67
Menu bar 13, 17, **18**
Microsoft Programs 13
  Access 13, 71, 97
  Excel 13, 71, **96-97**
  Office suite 13
  PowerPoint 13, 71, 97
Microsoft toolbar 71
Minimise button 17
monitor 11
More colours button 30
mouse 11, **13** *see* cursor
My Documents folder 22
My Pictures folder 22

N

Net *see* Internet
new document button 19
new web page button 100
newsletter 32, 38, 74,
    76-79
numbering
  lists 19, **39**
  pages 53, 77

O

Office Assistant 18
Office Suite 12
on-screen presentations 32,
    97
open Folder button 19
organising work 22, 67, 69
overtype mode 17, 67

P

page
  alignment **24-25**
  break 54
  layout 25
  margins 24
  moving around 13, 14, **17**
  numbers **53**, 77

odd/even 26, 53, 54
range (print) 25
set up 24-25
Page Down/Up keys 14
paper sizes *see* printing
paragraphs
alignment 36
format button 19
styling **36-37**
paste *see* cut
special 57
pencil shape cursor 49
pictures *see* images and illustrations
plain text format 23
posture 11
PowerPoint 13, 71, 97
preferences (general) 66-67
default 66
edit 67
spelling and grammar 58, 67
preview 25, 28, 30, 50
print button 19
printer 11, 25
printing 24-26
backgrounds 82
copies 26
double-sided pages 26
envelopes 24, 85, 86-89
ink cartridges 26
labels 86-89
layout view 72
margins and binding 24
odd/even pages 26
page set up 24-25
paper size 24
pause and stop/progress 26
photographic quality 24
preferences 67
preview 25
preview button 19, 25

Q

question mark icon 14
query options 97
quotations 36

R

radio buttons 25
Reading Layout 72
Redo typing button 19
reprint 26
repeating text 56
Return key 14, 20
ruler 17
columns **39**
indents **37**
tabs **41**

S

saving 22-23
button 19
different versions 23
documents **22**
preferences 67
Save as 22-23, 44-45
plain text 23
template 23, **44-45,** 79
web page 23, **100-102**
Screen tips 18
settings 66, *see* preferences
Scroll bars 17
scrolling 13, 17
search
for clips 75
for formatting 64
the web button 71
for words 64
selecting text 13
Shift key 14, 21
shortcut keys 13, **14**
view 18
Show/Hide invisibles button 19, **20**, 40, 54
sort
alphabetic **92-93**
numeric 92-93
sort options 92
Spacebar 14
spacing
characters **32**
lines **37**, **43**, 78

spelling and grammar 12, **58-59**
abbreviations 62
AutoCorrect 62-63
button 19
customise 58-59, 63
dictionary 59, 67
find and replace 63, 64
look up words 60-61
turn off 59
typographical errors 62
spreadsheets 48-49, **94-95**
cells 49, 94
formats 49
formulas 94-95
insert Excel button 19
Standard toolbar 16, **19**
stationery *see* labels
business 40, 42, 45, 50
envelopes 85, 86-89
form letters 85
invoice 40
letterheads 32, **42-45**
letters and faxes 13, **45**, 50, 63
templates **45**, 50-51
watermarks 82
Status bar 17
Style Gallery 47
styling documents 34-55, 77
see also formatting
new 35
options 12
options panel 19
preserving styles 47
text 28-32
styling text 28-32, 34
and Autocorrect 62
capitalisation 20
caps lock key 20
character scaling 32
drop cap 79
page numbers 53
paragraphs **36-37**
special effects 32
sum *see* calculations
synonyms and antonyms 60

T

tables 19, **48-49**, 92-93, 94-95
see lists databases, spreadsheets
AutoFit contents 48
borders 49, 53
cells 49, 93, 94
drawing 49
tabs 40-41 *see also* indents
leader lines 41
ruler 41
Taskbar 17
Task Pane 34, 60-61, 74-75, 84-89, 98
templates 19, 23, 35, 44-45, **47**, **50-51,** 69
document 19, 47
save document as 23, **44-45, 79**
using **50-51**
text *see also* fonts
AutoText 63
breaks 20, 38, 54
convert to table 93
delete **21**
enter **20**
hidden 31
hyphenation 37
justify 39
non-printing characters 20, 66
quotations 36
references 43
themes 35
track changes 67
wrap 20, 48, 54, 76, 81
Text box button 71
Themes 99
Thesaurus 60-61
Title bar 17, 23
toolbars 13, **68-71**
buttons 19, 44
clear 70
Clipboard toolbar 57
create 70
customise 66, 68-71
Drawing toolbar **71**, 80-81, 82
Formatting toolbar **19**, **34**, 37

Frames toolbar 101
Header and Footer toolbar 53
Microsoft toolbar **71**
Picture toolbar 75, 82
shortcuts 37
Standard toolbar 16, **19**
Web toolbar **71**
WordArt toolbar **71**
Tools menu 18
typefaces *see* fonts
typographical errors 62

U

underline
  button 19
  styles 31
undo 19, 47, 57
uploading 103
user preferences 67

V

view
  normal 72
  outline 72
  print layout 72
viewing
  buttons **17**, 72
  enlarge/reduce 72
  full screen 72
  multiple pages button 25
  options 72
  preferences 66
  screentips 18
  shortcut keys 18
  window, maximise 17
  zoom 19, 25, **72**
View menu 18, 72
viruses 91

W

Web
  address 98, 102
  address panel 71
  site 98, 102
Web page
  animated fonts 32
  backgrounds 82
  homepage 100
  hyperlink 19, 102
  layout view 72
  publishing 102
  sources 102
  styles 98
  template 13
  themes 35, 99-100
  toolbar 71
Window
  close 17
  document 17
  maximise/restore 17
  tidying 69, 70
  Title bar 17, 23
Windows key 14
Wizards 45, **50-51,** 98
Word
  description 12-13
  exporting **97**
  Help button 19
  opening 16
  versions 8,13, 97
  to Word 97
WordArt 80
  button 71
  Gallery 80
  toolbar 71
words
  counting **61**
  find and replace 63, **64**
  meanings 61
  synonyms and antonyms 60
  writing styles 59
work
  organising 22, 67, 69

Z

Zip disk 23
zoom 19, 25, **72**

For Reader's Digest

Editor
Caroline Boucher

Art Editor
Julie Bennett

Reader's Digest General Books

Editorial Director
Cortina Butler

Art Director
Nick Clark

Executive Editor
Julian Browne

Development Editor
Ruth Binney

Publishing Projects Manager
Alastair Holmes

Style Editor
Ron Pankhurst

This book was edited, designed and produced by

Planet Three Publishing Network,
Northburgh House,
10 Northburgh Street,
London EC1V 0AT

Editors
Eva Lauer
Gordon Torbet

Subeditors
Alan Brookes
Mary O'Sullivan
Jennifer Patterson
Mary Pickles
Laura Ward

Commissioning Editor
Jon Asbury

Art Editors
Gary Gilbert
Paula Keogh
Andrew Thomas
Michael Yeowell

Contributor
Lindy Newton

Authenticator
Tony Rilett

Acknowledgments

We would like to thank the following individuals and organisations for their assistance in producing this book.

Photography
Karl Adamson

Equipment
Epson, Hewlett Packard, Iomega, IQA, Key Tronic, Labtec

ISBN 0 276 44038 2
Book code 400-239-01
Oracle code 250009226S.00.24